The Ballymaloe Cook Book

MYRTLE ALLEN

Gill and Macmillan

Introduction by
LEN DEIGHTON

Drawings by
MEL CALMAN

Published in Ireland by
Gill and Macmillan Ltd
Goldenbridge
Dublin 8
with associated companies in
Auckland, Dallas, Delhi, Hong Kong,
Johannesburg, Lagos, London, Manzini,
Melbourne, Nairobi, New York, Singapore,
Tokyo, Washington
© Myrtle Allen, 1977, 1984
© Introduction, Len Deighton, 1977
© Drawings, Mel Calman, 1977
Second Impression 1984
0 7171 1339 6
Print origination in Ireland by
Keywrite Limited, Dublin
Printed by
Mount Salus Press Limited, Dublin

Contents

Foreword to the Second Edition

Since I wrote the first edition of Ballymaloe Cook Book, some new dishes as well as some classic old ones have made their way into our repertoire. So now it is time for a new edition which includes as much new material as possible. As before, I avoid recipes which we use in the restaurant but are to be found in other people's current publications. I must admit, however, that Jane Grigson's recipes are the basis for mine on pages 48, 50 and 151 for mussels, oysters and pastry cream.

Many years ago I took some lessons with Simone Beck in Paris. First of all, she searchingly asked me what cookery writers I read. When this was approved of, the lessons proceeded. Eventually, I dared to mention to her that I thought there was a little too much mustard in a recipe of hers for Lobster Thermidor. Her reply took me aback. She said, 'In Paris, it is no longer the fashion to put mustard in Lobster Thermidor.' On the strength of this precedent, I would like you to know that in Ballymaloe it is no longer the fashion to put roux in Irish Stew or so much treacle in Ballymaloe Brown Bread.

Fashion in food is more apparent as *Nouvelle Cuisine* sweeps through the smart kitchens of Europe. If I could start a fashion, it would be to recapture some forgotten flavours, or to preserve some that may soon die.

'The butter your sister is sending us is very good', I said to my neighbour one day. 'Yes', he said, 'that field always made good butter.' That is long ago and the fragrance is almost forgotten.

Ballymaloe House   Myrtle Allen
Shanagarry
Co. Cork
December 1983

Foreword to the First Edition

This is a collection of recipes in current use in my restaurant. Some are original as far as I know, if this is ever possible in cooking. Some are our adaptation of ordinary or traditional dishes. Others are classic recipes that we are frequently asked for.

Cooking is like a language. You hear other people speak, you taste what other people cook, you read what they have to say and then you go and do it yourself. Therefore these recipes are influenced by what has been said to my generation of cooks, from Soyer to Rosemary Hume, from Escoffier to David, including those three stalwarts from Paris, Beck, Bertholle and Child.

Acknowledgments

I would like to thank: My husband, Ivan. Nobody can cook well without somebody who will eat. The more discriminating the gourmet, the better the cook. Also my daughters-in-law, Hazel and Darina, for running the restaurant while I wrote my book, and the rest of my family and staff for their help in typing, testing and in many other ways. The late Rex Webster of Newtown School, Waterford. Paddy O'Keeffe and Larry Sheedy of the *Irish Farmers' Journal,* and also Patrick Staunton, who helped me to write and to publish. Len Deighton for his Introduction and his advice and encouragement. John Doyle of Dingle for information regarding the custom of making Dingle Pies. Mel Calman, Karen Usborne and Paul Mosse for illustrations and help. Philip Thompson, Quentin Doran-O'Reilly and Richard Eckersley who helped with design and layout.

Finally I wish to thank Michael Gill and his team, particularly Deirdre Rennison and Sarah Jackson, for their help and enthusiasm in compiling this second edition.

Introduction to the First Edition

Nowadays most cookery books turn out to be recipe books, just collections of formulae, and a selection of photos purchased from a photo-agency. Worse still, the recipes are all too often selected with the same reckless haste that the photos are chosen, and careful reading reveals them to be incompatible in method and style.

The reason for this sorry state of affairs — and I speak as a compulsive collector of cookery books — is simply that most of them are written by people who are primarily writers. For in the same way that few journalists have enough time to cook three meals a day, so few dedicated cooks have either the time or inclination to write a book about what they know. That is why it has taken a long time and much persuasion before Myrtle Allen finished this fine book: she is a professional cook.

The Allens have a hotel and restaurant not far from Cork in southernmost Ireland. It was not always a hotel. Once it was the home and grounds of the Allen family, who loved their house so much that they could not bear the idea of moving to a smaller one when their family grew up. So they turned the lower room into a restaurant, and gradually the rest of the house became a hotel.

I know of no better recommendation for a restaurant than a kitchen garden green with fresh vegetables and herbs. The Allens were market gardeners long before they opened their restaurant, and the cucumbers and the strawberries, the cauliflowers and mushrooms are all picked specially for each meal.

We all know of smart little restaurants where they make their own pork terrine, but at Ballymaloe they raise their own pigs and make everything from salt pork to sausages, not forgetting black puddings. A customer looking forward to crab or lobster would do well to speak to Myrtle in advance, for it won't have come out of the deep-freeze but out of the sea. Like the lobsters and the pork, lamb and beef will all be local produce.

But, as you will see from her book, getting the best ingredients is only the beginning, and Myrtle Allen is a wonderful cook. As well as telling us about Tommy Sliney, the fish man from nearby Ballycotton, and what happened to some difficult clients on the night that Paddy dropped the omelette, she tells us the secret of Ballymaloe's famous brown bread and gives us her recipes for Colcannon and Irish Stew.

So whether you read her book to learn a few things about running a restaurant, to reproduce some of her cooking, to enjoy her anecdotes or just to breathe a little Irish air, you will not be disappointed.

Len Deighton

Basic Information

Roux

In Ballymaloe, to make for greater speed and flexibility in cooking, all sauces are thickened with a pre-prepared roux. This consists of an equal weight of butter and flour, say 1 lb. or ½ kilo of each. The butter is melted and the flour cooked in it for 2 minutes on a low heat stirring occasionally. It is stored in a cool place and used as required. Alternatively, it can be made up on the spot in the usual way if preferred. It will keep at least a fortnight in a refrigerator. 85gr/ 3 ozs/¼ cup roux thickens 600 ml/1 pint/2½ cups liquid.

White roux and brown roux

The above method is for making a white roux which is the most useful for all purposes. A brown roux has a more nutty flavour and gives the sauce a darker colour. It is more suitable for gravies. To make the roux brown, increase the heat, stirring and watching carefully so that it does not blacken.

To thicken a sauce with roux

Bring the liquid to the boil, remove from heat and crumble in the roux. If it warms and softens in your hand a little, so much the better. Whisk it in vigorously and return to heat, still whisking. Do not add more roux before the liquid boils again as it will suddenly become thick at boiling point.

Equivalent terms

Irish	British	American
Bread soda	Bicarbonate of soda	Baking soda
Black treacle	Same	Molasses
Double cream	Same	Heavy cream
Flake meal	Porridge oats	Rolled oats flakes
Granulated sugar	Same	No equivalent, a coarsely ground sugar
Castor sugar	Same	Granulated
Icing sugar	Same	Confectioners or powdered sugar
Wholemeal flour	Same	Graham flour
Spring onion	Same	Scallion

This rule measures 6 inches or 152 millimetres

A 'young onion'
By this I mean any immature onion, still growing, with green leaves, usually bigger than a spring onion or scallion.

Bouquet garni
A sprig of parsley and thyme and a bay leaf tied together.

Butter
Unless otherwise stated, salted butter should be used for all recipes. If this is not possible add extra salt in any savoury recipe where the proportion of butter is high.

Gelatine
All recipes are for powdered gelatine.

Cheese
If no particular type is stated, a mild cheddar similar to the type made in Ireland is required.

Herbs
All recipes are intended for the use of fresh herbs. Substituting with a different herb is usually better than substituting with a dried herb.

Comparative Temperatures

Oven Temperatures	Fahrenheit	Centigrade	Gas Reg.
Cool & Very Cool	200°—300°	90°—150°	¼—2
Moderate	300°—375°	150°—190°	2—5
Moderate to hot	375°—400°	190°—200°	6
Hot	400°—475°	200°—240°	6—9

Measurements in Spoons

All spoon measurements are rounded unless otherwise stated, or if filled with a liquid.

Soups
and
Starters

KEVIN DUNNE

Cold Cucumber Soup

There are several versions of this good-tempered dish. It is easy to make, delicious to eat, and keeps for days. Try setting it in a ring mould with gelatine. Fill the centre with a bouquet of green leaves. Use a mixed bunch of pale lettuce leaves, watercress sprigs, spring onions and long sticks of cucumber. Hand French dressing separately. This is really best for a cold buffet. Individual moulds are a better starter.

Note on using gelatine: Put gelatine in a bowl. Add 1 tablespoon of cold or lukewarm water to the teaspoon of gelatine. Take a saucepan slightly smaller than the diameter of the top of the bowl. Put 1-2 inches/3-5 cm. water in it. Sit the bowl on top of the saucepan, it must not touch the bottom. Bring the water to the boil. Do not stir, but simmer until all the gelatine has dissolved. Always add a little of the liquid to be set into the gelatine bit by bit, stirring all the time. When mixed in, pour a spoonful into a saucer to cool to see if it is setting to the correct consistency. The setting quality of gelatine can vary according to the brand. The recipes in this book are for powdered gelatine.

Making Tomato Juice

After many experiments in trying to get a good tomato juice, I decided that nothing tasted better than the juice left from a tomato salad. I try to guess how much seasoning, herbs and French dressing I would put over some tomatoes and then I liquidise the lot. It's like playing tennis. If you have a good eye and concentrate on your shot you get a good result. Meanwhile, this recipe will get you started. If somebody talks to me in the middle, I do something awful like putting in two lots of vinegar.

The tomatoes must be almost at the point of ripeness when the skin will peel off without first scalding them.

Tomato Ring

Tomato juice set with gelatine in a ring mould is even better than a ring of Cold Cucumber Soup. Fill the centre with crab or egg mayonnaise. Omit the oil in the recipe.

Cold Cucumber Soup

Serves 8-10. Grate cucumber. Stir in all the other ingredients except the mint, which should be sprinkled on top just before serving. Serve chilled.

1 large cucumber
250 ml/8 fl oz/1 cup light cream
120 ml/4 fl oz/½ cup yoghurt
2 tablesp. tarragon vinegar
½ or 1 clove crushed garlic
1 tablesp. finely-chopped gherkins
2 tablesp. finely-chopped mint
salt and pepper

Cucumber Ring

Put gelatine and water in a bowl and hang over a saucepan of boiling water until melted. Blend carefully with the mixture. Can be kept chilled for a day or two.

15 g/½ oz/4 teasp. gelatine
1 tablesp. water
600 ml/1 pt/2½ cups cold soup

Tomato Juice

Serves approx. 5. Liquidise the ingredients together, then strain. Best when freshly made. Better not kept more than 12 hours. Boil up left-overs for a purée instead.

450 g/16 oz/2½ cups (roughly filled) peeled, halved, very ripe tomatoes
1 spring onion with a little green leaf
or
1 slice onion (5 cm/2 in dia., 7 mm/¼ in thick)
3 basil or mint leaves or a sprig of tarragon
2 teasp. white vinegar
1 tablesp. olive oil
120 ml/4 fl oz/½ cup cold water
1 level teasp. salt
1 level teasp. sugar
a few grinds black pepper

Tomato Ring

Make as for a Cucumber Ring, substituting Tomato Juice for Cold Cucumber Soup.

A Vinaigrette Starter

A difficult dish for parties and restaurant service as it cannot be made up in advance. It is so delicious it is worth organising some junior help to do the job, when it is needed.

Fruit Starters

Grapes, melon, grapefruit, oranges and tomatoes give a good juicy base for a fruit starter.

Chopped radish, celery, cucumber, watercress stalks, the crisp white top of a cauliflower or the dark purple bud of purple sprouting broccoli — all give a crunch. Use chopped peppers and spring onions with tomatoes.

Fresh mint, dill, thyme, lovage and basil, if you can get them, give aroma and flavour. Never use too much, though. Treat herbs with caution until you know them well.

These recipes can be made up to 12 hours in advance. If you keep them chilled, remember that a low temperature reduces flavour. You may want to warm them to room temperature before serving.

Cut each segment of grapefruit from inside its surrounding skin.

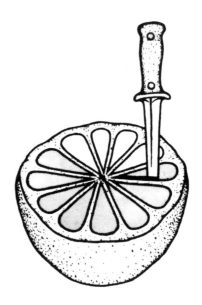

A Vinaigrette Starter

Peel and cut the tomatoes into quarters. Sprinkle them with salt, pepper and sugar. Put them in a cup and cover with French dressing. Cook asparagus and artichokes until just done. Peel the cucumber and cut into short sticks, 7 mm/¼ in thick. Sprinkle with salt and white vinegar. Wash the lettuce. Don't cut the avocado until the last minute. Leave all aside until ready to eat, then dip each item into the French dressing and arrange on a plate. Serve at room (not fridge) temperature.

Do not make up in advance as it all looks tired in 10 minutes.

For each person allow at least 3 of the following:
½ firm but ripe tomato
3 asparagus spears
2.5 cm/1 in cucumber
¼ ripe avocado
1 small globe artichoke
1 floret cauliflower lightly boiled
seasonings
French dressing
lettuce

Grapefruit, Lovage and Cucumber

Prepare the grapefruit as shown opposite. Add the cucumber. Crush lovage leaf in your hand to release the flavour. Put it to marinade with the fruit for 1 hour. Remove before serving. Decorate with another lovage leaf.

For each person allow:
½ grapefruit
1 level tablesp. coarsely-grated
  cucumber
¼ lovage leaf
lovage for decoration

Grape, Grapefruit and Celery

Prepare the grapefruit as shown opposite. Clean loose skin from fruit, to leave a smooth cup. Mix the segments with other ingredients. Fill back into skins for serving. Mint can be used instead of celery in summer-time.

For each person allow:
½ grapefruit
5 grapes
1 teasp. chopped celery
  or
pinch of chopped mint
1 level teasp. castor sugar

Grape and Melon Cocktail

Serves approx. 5. Squeeze the juice from the oranges and lemon. Stir in sugar. Scoop the melon flesh into balls with a potato baller. Scald, peel and remove pips from the grapes. Mix all together with a little finely-chopped mint and serve in individual glasses. Decorate with a fresh mint leaf. This looks very pretty using a few pink watermelon balls.

2 oranges
1 lemon
1 tablesp. castor sugar
½ medium-sized melon, very ripe
225g/½ lb grapes
sprig of mint

Persian Influences

The effect of climate on food fascinates me. It isn't just whether you have a gooseberry bush or a banana tree in the back garden: it is the moisture, the soil, herbs, winds and indigenous bacteria, that affect not only the kind but also the quality of food in different places.

I loathed yoghurt until I bought a plastic bagful from a nomad in the mountains north-west of Teheran. This was just something different again. All the learned men and expensive laboratories of north-west Europe cannot reproduce this type of yoghurt. No wonder. What it takes is a wild and tough man, backed by a herd of goats, a tribe of relations, a few earthenware jars and a vast area of barren mountainside, alternately roasting and freezing.

The Iranians know what they have got. They eat and drink it in every conceivable way. The best I could do when I got home was to take a Persian idea and adapt it to Irish materials.

The new concoction is not Persian and certainly not Irish. It is good in its own right for starting a gentle summer dinner. Use within 24 hours.

Note on Avocado Soup

This is very handy for using up avocados which are a bit too ripe to serve as they are, or to make a few go a long way. Keep chilled, use within 24 hours, if possible. Cover with plastic film, as the top becomes brown after some hours if left open to the air.

Persian Cocktail

Serves 6-8. Scald and peel the tomatoes. Peel the garlic and mash it to a paste with salt. Purée the tomatoes, garlic and salt together in a blender. Sieve out the pips if you wish. Add yoghurt. Stir in the mint. Serve chilled.

225 g/½ lb tomatoes
1 level teasp. salt
1 clove garlic
470 ml/16 fl oz/2 cups natural yoghurt
1 teasp. finely-chopped mint

Chilled Avocado Soup

Serves approx. 6. Peel the avocados. Grate the onion on a very fine grater and scrape up enough pulp to measure ½ teaspoon. Put with the remaining ingredients in a liquidiser. Reduce to a purée. Taste and add seasoning if necessary. Fill into small serving bowls and chill. Decorate the top with red pepper cut into fine shreds or tomato flesh, free of skin, cut into pretty shapes.

Note on tomato juice: Fresh juice is best. Alternatively, you could use, should you have any, the juices left over from a tomato salad, tomato fondue or a ratatouille. You could also just purée a few tomatoes, seasoning nicely with salt, pepper and sugar.

1 very ripe avocado
½ small onion
2 teasp. lemon juice
250 ml/8 fl oz/½ cup chicken stock
120 ml/4 fl oz/¼ cup very good French dressing
120 ml/4 fl oz/½ cup tomato juice
Garnish:
1 ripe tomato
or
½ red pepper

Chicken Stock

Essential for the Chilled Avocado Soup, and much the best for Lettuce, Spinach and Cucumber Soups. Shop around for the very best chicken bouillon or tinned consommé, or make your own as follows.

Put all ingredients into a saucepan. Bring to the boil and skim. Simmer for 3 hours. Strain and remove fat. If you need a stronger flavour, boil down the liquid in an open pan to reduce by ⅓ or ½ the volume.

1 large boiling fowl, disjointed
3½ l/6 pts/15 cups water
1 sliced onion
1 clove garlic
1 leek, split in two
1 stick celery or lovage leaf
1 chopped carrot
few sprigs parsley
6 peppercorns
2 teasp. salt

The Basic Soup

The basic system on the opposite page seems to produce a simple, homely kind of soup with a great many different vegetables. Just take whatever you have to hand and try it. It is wonderful with mixtures such as a cup of carrots, vegetable marrow, parsnips and cabbage. It has failed when the vegetables were not properly chopped, such as when whole spinach leaves were squashed into the cup. This threw out the proportions. I chop in rough 1 cm/½ in. dice and shred green leaves roughly the same way.

Note on Stock

Making stock need not be difficult or expensive; it can be just a method of working. Instead of throwing everything into a waste bucket or disposer, you keep a saucepan handy for suitable items. Put in vegetable parings, raw and cooked bones and carcasses, bacon rinds, parsley stalks, an onion, turnips and a few herbs. Exclude fish, green vegetables, bread, potato and excess of anything very strong such as bacon bones or poultry giblets.

Pack everything in and just cover with cold water — don't use too much — and a tight lid. Put on a very low heat. It should take about 30 minutes to come to the boil. Barely simmer for 8-12 hours. Then strain off the liquid.

Quantities

An estimate of numbers of servings must always be approximate. For instance, old ladies eat very much less than farm-hands. The soup I had worked out to serve nine people, just did two, when my son and his wife sat down to it.

Soup quantities are also governed by the amount of evaporation in cooking and in what you decide to add in milk or liaison afterwards. Allow 1 pint soup: 3 helpings; 1 litre: 5 helpings.

Party Quantities

Measure by the quart (1¼ l) instead of the cup. Multiply everything by five including the number of servings.

Note on Onions

From early summer to autumn, use freshly-picked onions. Use the bulb, the neck and some or all of the green stalk.

Basic Vegetable Soup

Serves 6. Melt butter in a heavy saucepan. When it foams, add potatoes and onions and turn them until well coated. Sprinkle with salt and pepper. Cover and sweat on a gentle heat for 10 minutes. Add the vegetables and stock. Boil until soft. Liquidise, sieve or put through a mouli. Do not overcook or the vegetables will lose their flavour. Adjust seasoning.

55 g/2 oz/4 tablesp. butter
110 g/4 oz/1 cup chopped onions
140 g/5 oz/1 cup chopped potatoes
340 g/12 oz/3 cups chopped vegetables of your choice
1 l/ 2 pt/5 cups stock
salt and pepper

Lettuce and Mint Soup

Serves approx. 6. Method as for Basic Soup. Add mint and cream at the end.
   Note: Good for using the coarse outer leaves of the lettuce, or a head that is starting to wilt or shoot.

110 g/4 oz/1 cup peeled diced onions
140 g/5 oz/1 cup peeled diced potatoes
1 teasp. salt approx.
freshly-ground pepper
170 g/6 oz/3 cups chopped lettuce leaves
1.2 l/2 pt/5 cups stock
2 teasp. freshly-chopped mint
1 tablesp. cream (optional)

Potato and Fresh Herb Soup

Serves approx. 7. Toss the potatoes and onions in hot butter and then sweat them on a gentle heat for 10 minutes, as in the Basic Soup recipe. Add stock and herbs and cook until soft. Remove tough herb stalks. Purée the soup, taste and adjust seasoning. Thin with creamy milk.

55 g/2 oz/4 tablesp. butter
110 g/4 oz/1 cup peeled diced onions
110 g/4 oz/1 cup peeled diced scallions
425 g/15 oz/3 cups peeled diced potatoes
1 teasp. salt
freshly-ground pepper
sprig of any 3 of the following: parsley, thyme, rosemary, lovage (1/2 leaf), bay-leaf (1/2 leaf)
1.2 l/2 pt/5 cups stock
250 ml/8 fl oz/1 cup creamy milk

Watercress

Watercress grows all over Ireland and Great Britain. A distinctive feature is that the top leaflet is rounded and larger than the side leaflets. This distinguishes it from *Apium nodiflorum,* a wild celery that grows with it, but is not dangerous to eat. It must not be picked in streams near grazing animals. For this reason, it is best to pick it beside a spring. It can be found all year round in County Cork, except during severe winters.

Watercress Soup

Serves approx. 6. Method as for Basic Soup. Water can be used instead of stock. Finally add yolk mixed with cream and do not boil again. Pour into bowls and garnish each helping with a teaspoon of whipped cream and place a watercress leaflet in the middle.

55 g/2 oz/4 tablesp. butter
110 g/4 oz/1 cup chopped onions
140 g/5 oz/1 cup chopped
potatoes
225 g/8 oz/5 cups chopped
watercress
½ l/1 pt/2½ cups water
½ l/1 pt/2½ cups creamy milk
1 egg yolk
1 tablesp. thick cream

Garnish:
2 tablesp. whipped cream
watercress leaflets

Carrot and Savoury Soup

Serves approx. 5. Heat the butter. Toss the carrot and onion in it until coated. Add a little salt and pepper and cover with a butter-wrapper, and then a tightly-fitting lid. Leave for 10 minutes on a low heat, to sweat gently. Remove the lid, add stock and boil until soft. Make into a purée. Taste and adjust seasoning. Add 2 teaspoons of savoury. Reheat when required. Garnish with a little whipped cream and sprinkle with the remaining savoury.

110 g/4 oz/1 cup sliced onions
285 g/10 oz/2 cups carrots
15 g/½ oz/1 tablesp. butter
900 ml/1½ pts/3¾ cups stock
salt and pepper
3 teasp. finely-chopped savoury
1 tablesp. whipped cream

Cucumber Soup

Serves approx. 6. Slice the cucumber and toss it in the hot butter. Add the onions and potatoes and cook, stirring, for 2 minutes more. Add stock, simmer until soft. Sieve, liquidise or put through a mouli. Just before serving, add the yolk, beaten into the cream.

1 cucumber
55 g/2 oz/4 tablesp. butter
110 g/4 oz/1 cup chopped onions
140 g/5 oz/1 cup chopped potatoes
1.2 l/2 pts/5 cups stock
1 egg yolk
1 tablesp. cream

Purée of Onion Soup

Serves approx. 6. Make as for Potato and Fresh Herb Soup.

55 g/2 oz/4 tablesp. butter
340 g/12 oz/3 cups chopped
onions
285 g/10 oz/2 cups chopped
potatoes
600 ml/1 pt/2½ cups stock
600 ml/1 pt/2½ cups creamy milk
sprig of thyme
salt and pepper

Note on Enrichments

All the purée-type of soups can be made by substituting milk for some of the stock, or by adding cream at the end. A liaison of egg yolk beaten into cream can be mixed in last thing. In a potato-based soup, it will curdle if boiled again, however.

Notes for Vegetarians

A meat stock gives a richness and flavour to soup. Without it you will need to add butter, cream, milk, egg or egg yolk and sometimes a vegetable savour, such as in the cauliflower soup. A cheese sauce with a generous amount of butter and cream in it makes a wonderful addition. Garnish with more grated cheese and crisply-fried, diced croûtons.

Note on Sweating Vegetables

If possible, use a heavy, cast-iron saucepan. Lay a butter-wrapper (buttery side down, of course!) on top of the vegetables to seal in the steam. Cover with a tight fitting lid.

French Peasant Soup

Serves approx. 5. Dice vegetables and bacon neatly before measuring. Cook bacon until the fat runs. Add potatoes, onions and crushed garlic. Sweat for 10 minutes. Add cabbage and tomatoes seasoned well with salt, pepper and sugar. Cover with stock and boil until the cabbage is soft. Taste and adjust the seasoning.

140 g/5 oz/1 cup streaky bacon
55 g/2 oz/½ cup onions
140 g/5 oz/1 cup potatoes
30g/1 oz/½ cup cabbage
185 g/6½ oz/1 cup peeled,
    chopped tomatoes
750 ml/1¼ pt/3 cups stock
1 clove garlic
salt and pepper
½ teasp. sugar

If we're not careful – we're going to end up in the soup..

Tomato Soups

Ripeness is all in a good tomato soup or purée. Unless the fruit is dark red, don't try it. Put the fruit to ripen in a warm place or better still shop around for over-ripe fruit. You might get them cheap. You certainly will if you live near a grower.

An ordinary old fashioned sieve is the best for making a tomato purée. It is essential to keep the skins out as they make the soup bitter. When you sieve tomatoes, do it thoroughly; the best part, the thick red flesh, is the last that can be pressed from the skins.

Tomatoes curdle milk, but not cream or a well boiled and thickened white sauce. Blend the purée and stock into the white sauce while it is still hot and freshly made.

Tomato Purée

1 kilo/2 lbs tomatoes should yield 600 ml/generous pint of purée. Put them in a saucepan with an onion and other ingredients. No water is needed. Cook over a slow heat until soft. Rub through a sieve.

1k/2 lbs ripe tomatoes
2 teasp. sugar
1 teasp. salt
grind of black pepper
1 onion

Tomato Soup

Serves approx. 5. Blend purée with sauce and stock. Taste carefully for seasoning. Dilute further if necessary. Bacon water is a good addition.
   Optional addition: some finely-chopped onions softened in butter.
   Garnish: whipped cream with chopped mint or basil.

750 ml/1¼ pt/3 cups tomato
   purée
250 ml/8 fl oz/1 cup white sauce
250 ml/8 fl oz/1 cup stock
1 tablesp. chopped onions
   (optional)
butter
mint or basil
120 ml/4 fl oz/½ cup whipped
   cream

Tomato Soup (party quantities)

Serves approx. 30 (35 using metric measures). Make a purée of the tomatoes, onions, herbs and seasonings. Dilute with stock and white sauce (relative proportions can be adjusted as convenient). Taste and adjust seasoning.

3k/6 lbs tomatoes
1 k/2 lbs onions
3 l/5 pts/12½ cups stock
2 l/3 pts/7½ cups white sauce

Quick Tomato Soup for 6

Sweat chopped onion in 30 g/1 oz/2 tablesp. butter. Peel the tomatoes, chop them up and add them with the herbs to the onions. Season with salt, pepper and sugar. Continue cooking gently until just done (8 minutes approx.). Add more butter if needed. Pour in stock, boil, liquidise and strain. Adjust seasoning. Add cream.

225g/½ lb tomatoes
1 tablesp. chopped onion
approx. 40g/1-2 oz/2-4 tablesp.
   butter
2 teasp. chopped herbs (thyme,
   tarragon, mint, basil)
600 ml/1 pt/2½ cups stock
175 ml/6 fl oz/¾ cup cream
salt and pepper

Thickening Soups

In the previous soups, potatoes thicken and suspend the particles of vegetable in the liquid. Otherwise, they would just form a sediment at the bottom of the pot.

In the following recipes flour is used instead of potato. It makes a smoother and more effective liaison.

Mushroom soup

The mushroom soup is best of all, when made with whole spring onions chopped in their entirety from the root to the tip of the green stalks. (But I do discard the root!)

Take care when blending the stock with the roux. Stir and beat well until it comes to the boil. Lumps of unblended roux are apt to lurk behind lumps of mushroom.

A little more stock and milk can be added carefully to taste, to increase quantities.

Cauliflower Soup

If you have to buy cauliflowers, you may have difficulty in getting untrimmed heads. Plenty of green leaves are essential to all the cooked cauliflower dishes in this book. Make a fuss — fight for them — somebody is wasting time, money and good food cutting them off and throwing them away. Look for a small independent greengrocer who buys direct from a garden.

Look out for second-grade cauliflowers for soup — frosted or shot heads will do fine and cost less.

Mushroom Soup

Serves approx. 4. Sweat onions in butter until soft (5 minutes approx.). Stir in mushrooms and seasoning and cook for 1 minute. Add flour and cook for 2 more minutes, stirring well. Remove from the heat. Blend in milk and stock. Return to the cooker and bring the mixture to the boil, stirring all the time. Adjust seasoning.

55 g/2 oz/4 tablesp. butter
2 tablesp. flour
110 g/4 oz/1 cup onions finely chopped
225 g/8 oz/2½ cups mushrooms finely chopped
salt and pepper
250 ml/8 fl oz/1 cup milk
250 ml/8 fl oz/1 cup stock

Artichoke Soup

Serves approx. 4. Peel and chop artichokes and onions. Sweat them in butter for 10 minutes. Remove from heat, sprinkle in flour. Beat in well and blend in stock. Put back on heat and cook until vegetables are soft. Stir occasionally. Sieve, mouli or liquidise. Return to heat and thin to required flavour and consistency with creamy milk. Adjust seasoning.
    Garnish: chopped parsley.

225 g/8 oz/1½ cups Jerusalem artichokes
110 g/4 oz/1 cup onions
30 g/1 oz/2 tablesp. butter
1 tablesp. flour
600 ml/1 pt/2½ cups light-coloured stock
300 ml/½ pt/1¼ cups creamy milk approx.
salt and pepper

Cauliflower Soup

Serves approx. 4. Wash the cauliflower. Take a quart of roughly-chopped green leaves and cauliflower stalks. Cover them with cold water, bring to the boil slowly and simmer for at least 20 minutes. Strain off the liquid. This gives you a cauliflower stock or savour. Chop up the cauliflower head with a few more leaves. Cover with the cauliflower stock and cook until tender. Sieve, mouli or liquidise. Measure the purée and add one-third its volume in a creamy cheese sauce. Reheat. Adjust seasoning.
    Garnish: 1 tablespoon grated cheese and 1 tablespoon finely diced croûtons of fried bread.

Approximate quantities:
1 small cauliflower with plenty of green leaves
600 ml/1 pt/2½ cups water
salt and pepper
350 ml/12 fl oz/1½ cups cheese sauce approx.

Turnip and Bacon Soup

Serves approx. 6-8. Cut the bacon into neat 1 cm/½ in dice and cook in a casserole until crisp. Squeeze out fat, remove bacon and reserve until later. Chop onions and potatoes, toss them in the fat and sweat for 10 minutes as in the Basic Soup recipe. Add stock and turnips. Cook gently until they are soft. Sieve, mouli or liquidise. Reheat when required.
    Garnish: chopped parsley and reserved bacon sprinkled on top.

140 g/5 oz/1 cup streaky bacon, rather fat
110 g/4 oz/1 cup chopped onions
140 g/5 oz/1 cup chopped potatoes
340 g/12 oz/3 cups chopped swede turnips
1 l/2 pt/5 cups stock
salt and pepper
1 tablesp. finely-chopped parsley

Crab Soup

Serves approx. 7.

200 g/7 oz brown and white crab meat, mixed
900 g/2 lbs fish skin and bones
255 g/9 oz carrots
255 g/9 oz onions
2 bay-leaves
4 sprigs of thyme
1 sprig of fennel
small bunch of parsley
few chives
15 g/½ oz/1 tablesp. butter
  or
1 tablesp. oil
2 medium-sized tomatoes
470 ml/16 fl oz/2 cups milk
30g/1 oz roux
1 teasp. salt
pepper
1 slice bread
butter and oil for frying croûtons

Fish stock
Slice up 85 g/3 oz carrots and 85 g/3 oz onions. Put them in a saucepan with one bay-leaf, a sprig of thyme, a few parsley stalks, the fish skin and bones and 1 1/2 pints/5 cups of cold water. Bring slowly to the boil and simmer for 20-30 minutes. Strain. Put 250 ml/8 fl oz/1 cup of this stock aside. Boil down the remaining stock to 600 ml/1 pt/2½ cups.

Vegetable base
Peel and slice the tomatoes. Slice 85 g/3 oz more each of carrots and onions. Heat butter or oil in a small saucepan. Add tomatoes, carrots, onions and fennel. Stir until coated with fat. Cover with a tight-fitting lid and sweat gently for 10 minutes. Add the reserved 250 ml/8 fl oz/1 cup fish stock. Boil until vegetables are soft. Blend to a purée.

White sauce
Slice the remaining carrots and onions and simmer them in the milk with parsley stalks, thyme and bay-leaf for 10-15 minutes. Strain out vegetables and slightly thicken sauce with roux. Season to taste.

To finish
Blend crab meat with fish stock. Add vegetable base and white sauce. Taste and adjust seasoning. Cut the bread into small cubes for croûtons. Fry in butter and oil until golden on all sides. They should be constantly tossed on a medium heat to avoid over-cooking on one side. Serve the soup with a garnish of these croûtons and plenty of finely-chopped parsley and chives.

Note: If you have already cooked your crab as described on page 38, you will have some crab stock left over. This can be added to the soup. Taste as you add to make sure it is not too strong.

Sauces

TIM ALLEN

Emulsion Sauces

So called because one has to emulsify oil with egg yolk. These two substances which normally reject each other have to be introduced gradually in very small quantities. If you go too fast they will part company and your sauce will curdle. The following emulsion sauces can discolour if made in an aluminium saucepan. They should be kept lukewarm and served as soon as possible.

To make Tarragon Vinegar and preserve Tarragon

If you can get fresh tarragon in summer, it is well worth picking and preserving for winter use. it is most abundant just before flowering in early August, so this is the best time to collect surplus growth.

There is no simpler preserve to prepare. Strip the leaves from the tarragon plants. Measure them and crush them in your hands. Put them in bottles and fill up with white malt vinegar. Allow 900 ml/1½ pt vinegar to 600 ml/1pt of crushed leaves. Cork the bottles and put away until required.

After 2 weeks the vinegar will be ready to use. The tarragon can be extracted from the bottom of the jar, chopped up finely and used in Béarnaise sauces throughout the winter.

Hollandaise Sauce

2 egg yolks
110 g/4 oz/½ cup butter
2 teasp. lemon juice

Serve with poached fish and eggs. Put yolks on a low heat in a heavy pan or in a bowl over hot water. Beat thoroughly. Add the butter bit by bit, in little pieces. As it becomes hot and thick, remove from heat. If it is slow to thicken, increase the heat. Do not leave the pan or stop beating until the sauce is made. Finally add lemon juice. If it gets too hot it will separate. This can be stopped in time by plunging the pan or bowl into cold water. If it happens, start again. This time add the sauce in teaspoonfuls to a tablespoon of iced water, off the heat, beating well. Keep lukewarm until service.

Béarnaise Sauce

Serve with grilled and roast meat and fish. If you do not have tarragon vinegar to hand, use a wine or malt vinegar adding extra chopped tarragon. Boil the first four ingredients together until completely reduced and the pan is almost dry but not browned. Add a tablespoon of cold water immediately. Put in egg yolks and make as for a Hollandaise Sauce, finally adding tarragon instead of lemon juice. Keep lukewarm until service.

pinch of ground black pepper
2 teasp. finely-chopped shallots
4 tablesp. tarragon vinegar
4 tablesp. dry white wine
1 tablesp. freshly-chopped
  tarragon leaves
  or
½ tablesp. dried tarragon
2 egg yolks
approx 150 g/4-6 oz/½-¾ cup
  butter

Sauce Beurre Blanc

Serve with fish and eggs. Boil the first four ingredients down to about ½ tablespoon. Beat in the butter in little pieces, keeping the sauce just warm enough to absorb the butter. Keep lukewarm until service.

3 tablesp. white wine
3 tablesp. white wine vinegar
1 tablesp. finely-chopped shallots
pinch of ground white pepper
170 g/6 oz/¾ cup butter

Mayonnaise

Serve with cold cooked meats, fowl, fish, eggs and vegetables. Have oil and yolks at room temperature. Mix half the vinegar, yolks and dry ingredients in a bowl. Whisk in the oil, ½ teaspoon at a time, until one-third of it is added; then add it 1 teaspoon at a time until two-thirds of it are added; then add it 1 tablespoon at a time. Beat well between each addition. When the sauce gets too heavy to beat, add remaining vinegar. If oil and yolks start to separate, start again beating the curdled mayonnaise, ½ teaspoon at a time, into 1 or 2 tablespoons of boiling water. If needed for coating, thin to required consistency with boiling water.

2 egg yolks
¼ teasp. salt
pinch of English mustard
  or
¼ teasp. French mustard
1 tablesp. white vinegar
250 ml/8 fl oz/1 cup oil

Garlic Mayonnaise

Serve with cold roast beef and fish. Make as for Mayonnaise, adding the garlic, well crushed, to the yolks. Fold in chopped parsley to finish.

ingredients as listed for Mayonnaise
1-4 cloves garlic
2 teasp. chopped parsley

Billy

Sometimes our chef, Billy, has his moments. One time, I noticed an amazingly good French dressing coming up from the kitchen. I went down to investigate. As he stuffed lots of herbs and seasonings into the blender, I rushed for a pen and paper to record what was going in.

Salad Dressing

Oil was not considered as a food in the average Irish household during the first half of the century. There was always a small glass bottle of rancid olive oil in our house, but it was kept in the medicine cupboard and used for sunburn. Cream dressings were served with salads. The traditional salad was and still is standard fare for Sunday evening suppers. It accompanied cold meat, probably left over from the midday joint. No dressing goes better with it than Lydia Strangman's, sister of my husband's elderly farming partner, an unmarried Quaker lady of strict principles, who spent her life painting and making a beautiful garden.

If you were an Irish tomato. how would you like to be smothered in foreign French dressing..

Billy's French Dressing

Put all the ingredients into a blender and run at medium speed for 2 minutes approx.

60 ml/2 fl oz/¼ cup vinegar
175 ml/6 fl oz/¾ cup oil
1 level teasp. mustard
1 large clove garlic
1 onion
sprig of parsley
sprig of watercress
1 level teasp. salt
few grinds of pepper

Lydia's Dressing

Sieve the egg yolks and add the sugar, salt and mustard. Blend in the vinegar and cream. Chop the egg whites and add some to the sauce. Scatter the rest over the salad. Do not dress the salad beforehand with this sauce: it will not coat the leaf. Hand it separately in a sauce boat.

2 hard-boiled eggs
¼ teasp. dry mustard
1 level teasp. salt
1 tablesp. soft brown sugar
1 tablesp. brown vinegar
4 tablesp. cream

White Sauce

Use as indicated in recipes. If using herbs and vegetables, put them into cold milk and bring to simmering point, season and simmer for 10-20 minutes. Remove pan from heat, remove the herbs and vegetables and crumble the roux into the milk. Bring to the boil, whisking until smooth, adding more roux if necessary. Adjust seasoning. If no herbs are used, bring milk to boil, with seasoning, add roux as described and simmer very gently for 5-7 minutes.

600 ml/1 pt/2½ cups milk
60 g/2 oz/¼ cup roux
salt and pepper
a few slices carrot
a few slices onion
bouquet garni

Enriched sauce
Stir in cream, or egg yolk, or a leftover Butter Sauce.

Cheese sauce
Beat in 110 g/4 oz/1¼ cups grated Cheddar cheese or 2 tablespoons of Gruyere cheese to a hot white sauce, quantities above.

Tartare Sauce

2 hard-boiled egg yolks
2 raw egg yolks
350 ml/12 fl oz/1½ cups olive oil
1-2 tablesp. vinegar
salt and pepper
1 teasp. chopped capers
1 teasp. chopped gherkins
2 teasp. chopped chives
  or
2 teasp. chopped spring onions
chopped white of egg

Serve with fried fish. Make as for Mayonnaise, mixing mashed hard-boiled egg with soft yolks. When finished, add flavouring.

French Dressing

1 tablesp. vinegar
3 tablesp. oil
salt and pepper

Mix seasoning with vinegar. Add oil. Shake well before use. A teaspoon of Mayonnaise added helps to keep the sauce in suspension for some time.

Cumberland Sauce

1 orange
½ lemon
225 g/½ lb redcurrant jelly
3-4 tablesp. port
pinch of cayenne pepper
pinch of ground ginger

Serve with cold meats, turkey, chicken, guinea fowl and game. Shred thin strips of rind from the orange and lemon, without any white pith. Simmer them in boiling water for 5 minutes approx. Squeeze the juice from the fruit and put it in a saucepan with the jelly and spices to melt down. Strain off water from shredded peel and add them with the port to the sauce. Boil rapidly for 5-10 minutes, when the sauce should set. It can then be potted and kept until needed, like jam.

Mint Sauce

1 tablesp. finely-chopped mint
2 teasp. sugar
3-4 tablesp. boiling water
1 tablesp. white vinegar

Put sugar and mint in a sauce boat. Add boiling water and vinegar. Allow to infuse 5-10 minutes before serving.

Bread Sauce

Serve with turkey, chicken and guinea fowl. Bring all the ingredients except cream to the boil in a saucepan. Cover and simmer gently in an oven or on top of the stove for 30 minutes. Remove the onions, and add cream before serving.

Note: Quatre Épices is a French product, a mixture of carefully-blended spices. It gives the best flavour to this very English sauce.

300 ml/½ pt/1¼ cups milk
150 g approx./5-6 oz/1½ cups breadcrumbs
1 onion stuck with 6 cloves
30 g/1 oz/2 tablesp. butter
salt and pepper
¼ teasp. quatre épices
1 tablesp. thick cream

Horse-radish Sauce

Serve with roast beef. Mix all ingredients together.

250 ml/8 fl oz/1 cup whipped cream
2 teasp. vinegar
1 teasp. lemon juice
¼ teasp. mustard
¼ teasp. salt
pinch of pepper
1 teasp. sugar
1½ tablesp. grated horse-radish

Redcurrant Jelly

Serve with cold meats, turkey, chicken, guinea fowl and game. Cover fruit with cold water. Bring to the boil and cook for about 5 minutes until fruit is soft. Turn into a strainer placed over a bowl. Leave to stand for 10 minutes approx. Do not press fruit or juice will become cloudy. Measure the juice. For every 600 ml/1 pt/2½ cups juice allow 450 g/1 lb sugar. Boil juice and sugar together rapidly until setting point is reached. This will take 5-10 minutes. Put a teaspoon of the liquid on a saucer in a fridge to test for a set. Pot and cover as for jam. It will keep a year in a cool dry place.

Note: The fruit can be rubbed through a sieve afterwards, well sweetened and mixed with some whipped cream and stiffly-beaten egg whites. Serve as a sweet with shortbread biscuits. It will have lost some of its flavour, however.

fresh or frozen redcurrants
sugar
water

The End of the Season

At the end of the season, the tomato plants in our glass-houses are tall and leggy, stripped of saleable fruit and leaves after the summer season. The remaining leaves and the last ripening trusses are at the top of the plant, too high for me to reach, but the lower stalks are not completely bare. Lovely sprays of firm ripe cherry tomatoes, too small for commercial people to bother with, are left behind by the pickers.

I discovered that by altering my tomato chutney recipe, I could make a lovely sauce with the whole tiny fruit, using the ripest of them, even if they were soft.

Spiced Tomato Sauce

Makes approx. 900 g/2 lbs sauce. Put the tomatoes in a bowl and cover with boiling water. Steep 2 minutes approx., then slash the skin and squeeze. The fruit should pop out, leaving the empty skin in your fingers.

In order to keep a good red colour, boil the tomatoes with all the other ingredients, except the green peppercorns, in a wide shallow pan for rapid evaporation. When reduced to about one-half, add the peppercorns and cook for another 5 minutes. It should be thick. Pot into jam jars and cover as for jam. The sauce should keep for 6 months or more. Serve with cheese or cold meats.

Note: White wine and red vinegar can be used instead of red wine and white vinegar.

900 g/2 lbs very ripe tomatoes, preferably cherry tomatoes
140 g/5 oz/1¼ cups onions, sliced
285 g/10 oz/1¼ cups sugar
2 teasp. salt
1 level teasp. allspice
300 ml/½ pt/1¼ cups red wine
300 ml/½ pt/1¼ cups white wine vinegar
1 teasp. mashed green peppercorns

Tomato Chutney

Skin the tomatoes and chop the shallots. Put all the other ingredients in a saucepan and bring to the boil. Add the tomatoes and shallots and simmer slowly without a lid, until thick. Pot and keep like jam.

1.35 k/3 lbs ripe tomatoes
450 g/1 lb/2 cups sugar
250 g/½ lb shallots
110 g/¼ lb/¾ cup sultanas
1 tablesp. salt
1 teasp. pepper
7 g/¼ oz/3 level teasp. mustard seed
½ teasp. allspice (pimento)
900 ml/1½ pt/3¾ cups vinegar

Fish and Shellfish

KEVIN DUNNE

Crabs and Lobsters

Somebody once said that the best way of killing a lobster was to run a knife through the cross on the top of its head provided you were married to a butcher or a commando (Monica Sheridan writing in the *Irish Times).* I first witnessed the ordeal at a demonstration in Paris. The fish in question was what we call a crayfish, their 'spiney lobster', and he, like me, had just arrived in this strange country from the south coast of Ireland, so I really felt an affection for him. Well, cruelly murdered he was, and I am simply not willing or able to kill a lobster in that way. Neither can I bear to plunge them into a pot of boiling water.

I follow hopefully the theory that crabs and lobsters die painlessly in slowly warming water. I hope this way is easier on their nerves; it's certainly easier on mine.

I put the fish in a saucepan with warm water, about the same temperature as a rock pool in summer (although they would probably prefer rather deeper water). With luck he will relax. Then the pot goes on a low heat and the fish collapses and dies at a low temperature, about 112°F(44°C).

For crabs, I pour most of the water away at this stage and steam them until they are cooked through. Lobsters and crayfish are also removed and steamed in a court bouillon, or are ready in the raw stage for many of the classic lobster dishes.

Catch a live crab like this if you don't want to lose a finger.

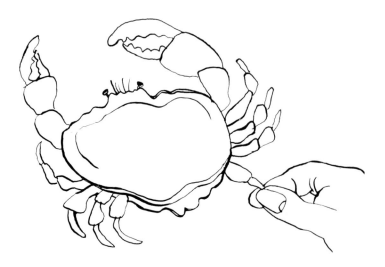

A lobster like this.

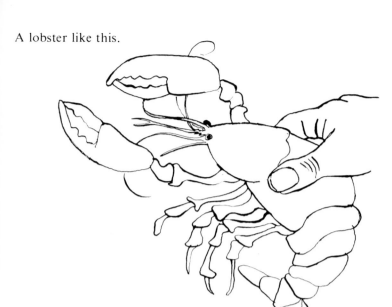

Drop it into a saucepan of lukewarm water — like a rock pool in summer; he should relax but sometimes splashes. Warm the water slowly — he should fall asleep.

Remove claws first. Plunge knife in here. Dark green juice will scramble to a beautiful coral in hot butter. Use all soft meat. Throw away gills and sac (stomach bag).

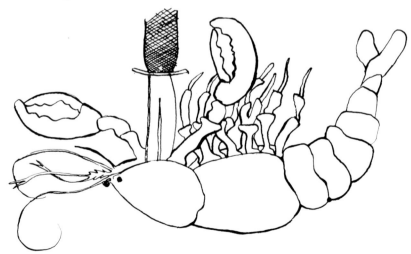

Opening a Raw Lobster

Dark green juices may run from the head as you cut it open, so lay the lobster upside down on a chopping board placed inside a shallow dish or tray. Plunge the point of a strong knife near the head. Work the point of the knife back down the tail, cutting right through the centre and scoring the shell underneath if you cannot actually cut through it. Take a half shell in each hand and crack apart into two halves. Carefully remove the claws, taking care that the body shell does not break away from the tail. Remove the stomach bag which should lie just above your first cut, and the intestine that runs down the tail.

Hot Buttered Lobster is simple in the extreme and like all simple dishes the rules should be followed meticulously. For the finest results, the meat should not be allowed to get cold. It is half-cooked in a court bouillon and kept warm until the cooking is finished in butter.

Desperation Rewarded

I was really stuck one night — not enough crab to go round and customers in the dining-room demanding it. Toast, onions and tomatoes would spin it out, I thought in desperation.

Success! I was summoned to the dining-room to present my recipe to an American guest. I had to think what I had done and scribble it hastily on a postcard. A month later he sent me back a photostat copy of my postcard. At that stage I thought I had better do it again.

A Gourmet Arrives

A gourmet was arriving for supper unexpectedly. In those days we had no restaurant. Fortunately it was low tide, so I hurried to the spot where our small but clean country stream runs over the strand. I gathered the few small mussels which were stuck to the rocks that obstruct its path. On my way home I thought I would stuff them with buttery crumbs mixed with garlic and parsley like the snails I had eaten in Paris.

We sat down to the meal, 'Ah' he said, 'Moules Farci!' Well, I thought, so that's what they call them!

Opening Mussels

Scrub them well. Put them, one or two shells deep, in a pan on a low heat. Cover with a cloth. They will open in the steam. They are moist, juicy and almost raw, if you catch them at the first moment of opening. At this stage they are indeed the poor man's oyster. Eat them with mayonnaise and brown bread. The longer they cook the smaller and more leathery they become.

Each shell has a fibrous tuft, called the beard, protruding from the middle of the straight edge. It must be removed after opening.

Hot Crab Hors D'Oeuvre

Serves approx. 4. Soften onion in butter. Remove from the pan. Peel and slice the tomatoes. Season them with salt, pepper and sugar, and also soften in butter, but not for too long. Chop finely some chives and parsley and mix with thyme leaves. Prepare some buttered toast. Lay the tomatoes on the toast. Sprinkle them with onions and then with the fresh herbs. Spread the dressed crab over this mixture and heat through under a grill.

155 g/5½ oz/1 cup dressed crab
2 tomatoes
1 chopped onion
salt, pepper, sugar
30 g/1 oz/2 tablesp. butter
1 tablesp. mixed chopped parsley, thyme and chives
4 slices toast

Stuffed Mussels

Serves 5 or 6 (2 or 3 main course). Open the mussels. Remove the beard and discard a half shell from each. Melt the butter and soak it up with crumbs. Mash garlic with a little salt to a paste. Add it to the crumbs with the parsley. Loosely fill the shells with this mixture and brown them under a grill.

955 g/2 lb 2 oz/5 cups scrubbed mussels (weighed in shells)
45 g/1½ oz/3 tablesp. butter
100 g/4 oz approx/1 cup soft breadcrumbs
1 tablesp. chopped parsley
1 clove garlic

Moules Marinière

Serves 5 or 6 (2 or 3 main course). Steam open the mussels with the wine and herbs. Remove a half shell and the beard from each. They can be kept at this stage for some time, even for a day or two in the fridge, as long as they sit in the cooking liquid.
Service: Heat the cooking juices. When boiling, add the fish, allowing them to heat through but not to cook any more. Remove from the heat and stir in Hollandaise sauce. Serve at once.

955 g/2lb 2 oz/5 cups scrubbed mussels (weighed in shells)
2 teasp. chopped parsley
2 teasp. chopped spring onions
1 teasp. chopped thyme leaves
1 teasp. chopped chives
½ teasp. chopped fennel
455 ml/16 fl oz/2 cups dry white wine
1 tablesp. Hollandaise sauce

Coping with Crabs

Choose heavy crabs. Those caught by potters off the rocks are better than those caught in a trawl off a sandy bottom.

Crabs will steam in about 20 minutes. Leave them the right way up to drain and cool.

First remove the claws. Crack them and take out the white meat. Be careful to keep out splinters of hard shell and clear all the debris away before you start on the rest.

Prise the body away from the back. I always do this by holding the crab upside down and levering off the lower part on the edge of the kitchen table. Scoop out all the meat from the shell, having first removed the stomach bag or sac.

The insides of crabs vary enormously, but no matter how deadly they look they are almost always alright provided the crab was alive in the first place. I only discard the ones that consist of pure black liquid. In a good crab, more meat can be picked from the body. Watch for the grey feathery lung which must also be discarded.

Mix body and claw meat together.

The simplest way to serve is to mix with an equal quantity of mayonnaise and a very little finely grated onion, with brown bread and butter to hand.

Engarde!

Crab Mayonnaise on Brown Bread

Serves approx. 4-6. Mix crab meat with mayonnaise and onion. Heap the mixture onto some slices of brown bread, decorating with plenty of lettuce or cress.

Crab Mayonnaise is the best filling for a tomato ring.

140 g/5 oz/1 cup crab meat
175-250 ml/6-8 fl oz/¾-1 cup
 mayonnaise
½ teasp. finely-grated onion
brown bread and butter
small lettuce leaves
 or
garden cress
 or
watercress

Dressed Crab

Serves 5-6 main-course helpings. Scrub the crab shells. Mix all the ingredients together. Taste for seasoning. Pack into shells. Top with buttered crumbs. Bake in a moderately-hot oven until heated through and brown on top, 20 minutes approx. at 200°C/400°F/Regulo 6.

Note: 450 g/1 lb cooked crab, in the shell, yields 110-170 g/4-6 oz approx. crab meat.

425 g/15 oz/3 cups crab meat (2
 or 3 crabs should yield this)
170-200 g/6-7 oz/1½ cups soft
 breadcrumbs
½ tablesp. white vinegar
2 tablesp. chutney
30 g/1 oz/2 tablesp. butter
generous pinch of dry mustard
 or
1 level teasp. French mustard
salt and pepper
120 ml/4 fl oz/½ cup white sauce
110 g/4 oz/1 cup buttered
 crumbs

Prawns and Scallops

Apart from crabs, lobsters, and oyster beds, this coastline does not favour shellfish. We get them from the deep bays off the west coast. There is also a fine organisation working there. If I telephone for fish in the morning, the previous night's catch is on my table for the evening meal.

The scallop recipe makes a good filling for Vol-au-Vents or Bouchées. It can also serve as a stuffing for flat fish.

De-veining Prawn Tails

Take the tail fin between your first finger and thumb, pinch it tightly and wriggle it up and down until the shell breaks. Pull slowly and steadily. If the prawn is fresh the gut will come away. This will not work with cooked prawns but it does with home-frozen prawns, provided they are put in very fresh. One month is long enough to keep them in a deep freeze. For this period, you can put them in without first shelling them. It is nicer to have de-veined prawns but only essential in the tropics.

Boiling Prawns

Use barely enough boiling salted water to cover (1 teaspoon salt to 600 ml/1 pt/2½ cups water). Once in, you must watch the pot until they are cooked. With a big quantity this happens before the water has even come back to the boil. Allow ½-1 minute at boiling point. Over-cooked prawns are a disaster.

Scallops with Cream and Mushrooms

Serves approx. 4 (2 main course). Choose a frying pan that just fits the scallops in one layer. Fry chopped onion in butter for 1-2 minutes. Add the chopped scallops and continue cooking for another couple of minutes. Half cover them with cream, season and cover the pan; leave on a low heat for 5 minutes. Fry sliced mushrooms lightly in butter in a separate pan and then add them to the scallops with their cooking juices. Thicken the sauce with roux, adding more cream if necessary. Taste it. Add parsley, lemon juice and adjust seasoning.

1 tablesp. finely-chopped onion or shallot
45 g/1½ oz/3 tablesp. butter
4 large scallops, chopped
250 ml/8 fl oz/1 cup light cream
110 g/¼ lb sliced button mushrooms
1 teasp. butter
roux
salt and pepper
lemon juice
½ tablesp. chopped parsley

Buttered Prawns with Herbed Hollandaise Sauce

Serves approx 4 (2 main course).

Herbed Hollandaise sauce: Mix egg yolk, mustard and herbs. Boil 85 g/3 oz/6 tablesp. butter and pour it in a thin stream onto the yolks, beating all the time.

De-vein, boil and shell the prawns. Toss them in remaining foaming butter, until heated through. Heap onto a hot serving dish, coat with Herbed Hollandaise Sauce and garnish with triangles of hot buttered toast.

1 egg yolk
½ teasp. French mustard
1 tablesp. mixed finely-chopped chives, fennel, parsley, thyme
140 g/5 oz/10 tablesp. butter
450 g/1 lb prawn tails
2 slices hot buttered toast

Ways with all Fish

Almost all the methods and sauces are interchangeable with different kinds of fish, so use your own taste and discretion. Mushrooms sliced and lightly fried in butter, with lemon juice added last thing; fresh herbs; dry white wine; a garlicky sauce; a Hollandaise type of enrichment: all add another dimension to your dish.

Garlic Butter: Beat mashed garlic and chopped parsley into butter. For herrings, add French or English mustard.

Quick Hollandaise: Put an egg yolk in a cup with salt and pepper. Boil 60 g/2 oz/4 tablesp. butter and pour it onto the egg yolk in a thin stream, while you beat with a fork. Add lemon juice to taste. Add herbs for a Herbed Hollandaise.

Buttered Crumbs are a useful topping and the basis of various fish and meat stuffings. Mix 110 g/4/oz/1 cup soft crumbs with 30 g/1 oz/2 tablesp. melted butter.

Aromatic Herbs for Fish: Parsley, Bay, Fennel, Dill, Thyme, Chives.

Aromatic Vegetables for Fish: Celery, Carrots, Onions, Turnips, Tomatoes (sometimes).

Look out —
Myrtle's got fresh fish
on the menu tonight

Hot Buttered Lobster

Serves 4. Kill the lobsters as described. Slice carrot and onion and put with wine, water and herbs into a saucepan and bring to the boil. Put in the lobsters, cover with a tight-fitting lid. Steam them until they are beginning to change colour and speckle with red. Remove pot from heat and leave aside, still covered, until you wish to eat them. Keep the cooking water for a sauce or soup. It will take you 5 minutes approx. to extract the meat from each fish. Open the lobster and put the meat from body, tail and claws and all green juices into a warm bowl wrapped in a tea-towel. Heat the lobster shells. Toss meat and green juices into hot foaming butter until the meat is cooked through and juices turn pink. Use plenty of butter and only cook one helping at a time. Spoon meat back into hot shells. Put the remaining butter into the pan, heat and scrape up any remaining bits. Pour into a hot sauce boat or individual heated butter dishes. Serve with quartered lemon and green salad.

Hot Buttered Lobster has to be eaten immediately. But if you put it in a sauce made from the pan juices, it can be kept for a day or two and reheated. See next recipe.

1.8 k/4 lbs live lobsters
1 carrot
1 onion
600 ml/1 pt/2½ cups water
600 ml/1 pt/2½ cups dry white wine
herb bouquet
170 g/6 oz/1¾ cup butter approx.
1 lemon

Lobster with Fresh Herbs and Cream

Sauté mushrooms in butter for about a minute. Add lemon juice. Set aside. Toss semi-cooked lobster meat in foaming butter as described in previous recipe. Remove and then cook shallot in the same pan. After approx. 2 minutes, add the white wine and reduce by half. Now add lobster cooking water and boil down again. Pull the pan aside and thicken with beurre manie or roux. Boil and stir. Remove from the heat again, add mushrooms and blend in cream. Boil up sauce for the last time, taste for seasoning and stir in the herbs and Hollandaise or Béarnaise sauce. Stir in lobster meat. Fill back into heated shells and brown the top under a grill. If you add 60 g/2 oz/½ cup grated cheese to the sauce and sprinkle more on the top, you can call this dish Lobster Mornay.

For each person allow:
140 g/5 oz/1 cup lobster meat
2 teasp. finely-chopped shallot
120 ml/4 fl oz/½ cup dry white wine
120 ml/4 fl oz/½ cup lobster cooking water
110 g/¼ lb sliced button mushrooms
butter and roux
1 teasp. lemon juice
120-250 ml/½-1 cup cream
1 teasp. thyme leaves
1 teasp. chopped parsley
2 teasp. Hollandaise or Béarnaise sauce

A Mousseline of Mussels and Seakale

955 g/2 lb 2 oz/5 cups mussels
   (weighed in shells)
2 egg yolks
100 g/4 oz/½ cup unsalted butter
2 teasp. lemon juice
120 ml/4 fl oz/½ cup whipped
   cream
450 g/1 lb seakale

Asparagus, globe or Jerusalem artichokes can be used instead of seakale.
   Serves approx. 4 as a first course. Cut the seakale into sticks 5 cm x 7 mm/
2 in x ¼ in approx. Boil them in a little unsalted water. Make a Hollandaise
sauce with the yolks, butter and lemon juice. Open the mussels. Strain the
juices through muslin or a filter paper, put in a saucepan and boil down to 3
tablespoons. Stir this reduction into the Hollandaise. Add whipped cream.

Remove the mussels from their shells, heat them in any remaining juices or
in a little seakale water. Arrange the seakale on individual plates or a serving
dish. Scatter the mussels over them and spoon over the sauce. Serve
immediately.

Note: As well as giving lightness to this sauce, the whipped cream coun-
teracts the salty flavour of the reduction, so add more if necessary.

Plaice Stuffed with Mussels

900 g/2 lbs fish fillets
900 g/2 lbs mussels
1 teasp. roux
ingredients as listed for Moules
   Marinière
ingredients as listed for Stuffed
   Mussels

Serves approx. 4. The fillets are sandwiched together with thickened Moules
Marinière mixture and topped with Stuffed Mussels mixture.

Steam open the mussels with wine and herbs. Discard all shells. Strain off
liquid. Boil and thicken slightly with roux. Remove from heat. Add Hollandaise sauce and mussels. Sandwich fillets with this mixture. Sprinkle the
top with crumbs prepared as for Stuffed Mussels. Bake until cooked through
and the crumbs are nicely browned in a moderately-hot oven, 200°C, 400°F,
Regulo 6.

Mayonnaise for Mussels, Cockles and Other Small Shellfish

1 egg yolk
¼ teasp. salt
½ clove garlic
½-1 teasp. vinegar
½-1 teasp. lemon juice
120 ml/4 fl oz/½ cup oil

Sufficient for approx. 50 shells (1.2 l/½ pt/5 cups mussels). Put the egg yolk in
a small bowl with the vinegar and lemon juice. Peel garlic and crush it in the
salt, then add it to the yolk. Whisk in the oil, ¼ teaspoon at a time, until one-
third of it is in. Beat well between each addition. Increase to 1 teaspoon at a
time, and continue increasing the quantity until all the oil is in.

Check the seasoning; thin to the consistency of thick cream with the juices
from the shellfish. Fill each shell to the top with this mayonnaise and
sprinkle with finely-chopped parsley. Serve with plenty of brown bread and
butter.

Cockles Au Gratin

Serves approx. 4. Wash cockles in several changes of cold water, then leave them in a colander under a running cold tap to remove sand. Open them in a pan containing onion, parsley, wine, water and a little ground pepper. Remove the fish from the shells, saving all the liquid. Boil the liquid for 1-2 minutes. Thicken with roux and add an equal quantity of cream. Test for seasoning. Salt may not be necessary. Stir fish into the sauce and fill the shells with mixture. Top with a pinch of grated cheese.

1240 g/2 lb 12 oz/7½-10 cups cockles (weighed in shells)
½ tablesp. finely-chopped onion or shallot
2 teasp. finely-chopped parsley
120 ml./4 fl oz/½ cup dry white wine
120 ml/4 fl oz/½ cup water
roux
black pepper
250 ml/8 fl oz/1 cup cream approx.
55 g/2 oz/½ cup finely-grated cheese

Sea Urchins

Serves approx. 4. Treat them rather like a boiled egg. Cook for 3-4 minutes in boiling water. Remove prickles from the top of the shell. Lever out the plug with the point of a kitchen scissors. Cut a large hole. Scoop out the meat, sieve it and mix it with mayonnaise. Fill back and serve with fingers of toast.

12 sea urchins
2 tablesp. mayonnaise
2 slices buttered toast

Shellfish Salad

Raw mussels, chopped cooked scallops and prawns go well in this salad. Mix all ingredients together and serve with lettuce or a tomato salad.

Allow per person:
75 g/2½ oz/⅓ cup cooked long-grained rice
75 g/2½ oz/⅓ cup shellfish
1 teasp. French dressing
little crushed garlic
½ teasp. lemon juice

Taramasalata

Peel and crush garlic with a little salt. Blend all ingredients together. Serve with lettuce and toast or brown bread.

Allow per person as starter:
900 ml/3 fl oz/⅓ cup smoked cod or hard herring roe (mash before measuring)
2 teasp. oil
2 teasp. lemon juice
little crushed garlic
pinch of salt

Sea Urchins, Shellfish Salad and Taramasalata are three good cold fish dishes. They make a pleasant starter for dinner.

Opening Oysters

Place the oyster on a tea-towel, flat side up. Wrap your left hand in another cloth so that you do not get cut if the knife slips. Take your oyster knife in your right hand. A chisel will have to do if you don't have an oyster knife. Look for a chink or crevice in the shell at the narrow, hinged end. Insert the blade and press, turn, and lever upwards. Use all your strength and keep at it — it will open. Insert a clean knife and cut the oyster away from the top shell. Serve immediately, chilled, with wedges of lemon.

I know what to do with shot cauliflowers, soft tomatoes, old hens and scraps of fat meat. I enjoy using what the world discards. My best find was damaged cooking oysters.

Champagne Sauce

This recipe comes from Jane Grigson's *Fish Cookery*. It makes a wonderful sauce for oysters, as she suggests, and also for poached grey mullet.

Fish Pâté

A fish pâté or potted fish makes a wonderfully easy lunch or supper dish. Packed into tiny individual pots, a selection of any three makes a stunning dinner party starter. They are not suitable for picnics, unless packed in a chilled container, as the butter goes soft.

Hot Buttered Oysters

Allow per person:
4-6 oysters
15 g/½ oz/1 tablesp. butter
1 slice buttered toast
1 slice lemon

Open the oysters, reserving their liquid. Heat half the butter until it foams. Toss the oysters in this until hot through, 1 minute perhaps. Put them on the toast. Pour reserved liquid into the pan and boil up, adding the remaining butter. Pour over toast and serve immediately with a wedge of lemon.

Champagne Sauce

½ bottle champagne or dry
sparkling white wine
30 g/1 oz/1 tablesp. chopped
shallot
4 large egg yolks
225 g/8 oz/1 cup butter
300 ml/½ pt/1¼ cup double
cream

Boil the wine with the shallot, reducing down to 1 tablespoon approx. Cool and beat in the yolks. Add butter, bit by bit, over a very low heat, as for Hollandaise sauce. Fold in the whipped cream.

Potted Shrimps or Lobster

Serves 4 (first-course). Crush garlic to a paste with a little salt. Bring butter to the boil with thyme leaves and garlic. Add shrimps and simmer together 3-5 minutes. Season carefully with 1 or 2 teaspoons of lemon juice. Pack into pots and run more melted butter over the top.

½ clove garlic
55-85 g/2-3 oz/4-6 tablesp.
* butter*
1 teasp. thyme leaves
110 g/¼ lb shelled shrimps or
diced lobster meat
2 teasp. lemon juice
salt and pepper

Potted Crab

Blend all the ingredients together. Pack into pots. Run melted butter over the top.

140 g/5 oz/1 cup mixed brown
* and white crab meat*
110 g/4 oz/½ cup softened butter
2 teasp. finely-chopped parsley
1 medium clove garlic, crushed
few grinds of black pepper
2-4 teasp. spiced tomato sauce,
* tomato chutney or mango*
* chutney*

Salmon or Mackerel Mousse

Blend all the ingredients together. Pack into little pots or a loaf tin. If using pots, run melted butter over the top. Chill well before serving. It will not keep for more than 3 or 4 days.

110 g/4 oz lb cooked fish, free of
* skin and bone*
55-85 g/2-3 oz/4-6 tablesp.
* softened butter*
¼ teasp. finely-snipped fennel
½ teasp. lemon juice
½ clove garlic, crushed to a paste

Smoked Mackerel or Smoked Salmon Pâté

Remove skin and bones from the fish. Weigh the flesh. Add three-quarters the weight in butter. Blend to a smooth purée. Fill into pots and run clarified butter over the top. Alternatively, mould in a loaf tin. Turn out and cut in slices when set.

smoked mackerel or salmon
softened butter

Opening a Restaurant in Paris

I got there, as it were, by mistake.

I had the idea of starting an Irish restaurant in Paris, when I was in Brussels. I was doing an Irish food fortnight at a big hotel there. Irish food, Irish cooking? Well, they'd had French, Chinese, Scandinavian, Italian, Russian, Indian and American food, and appeared to be bored by the lot. I'll swear they actually *needed* brown soda bread. Apple cakes made with Bramley's seedlings, good old Irish bacon and sausages and Irish stew took on a new air of being rather special.

Quite a few years later, a tortuous route brought me to the situation on this particular August morning. We were packed with guests at Ballymaloe, and packed with young cooks chasing in and out between the stores and two loaded cars in the courtyard. The last few precious items were thrown in amongst the apples, potatoes, fabrics, suitcases and floor cloths, a skimming bowl, a few pounds of tea, somebody's jersey. Cameras clicked. The young staff tearfully embraced, and off half of them went to catch the boat for France. The other half went sadly back to work in Ballymaloe kitchen. A week later I flew out after them to re-open the Irish restaurant in Paris.

Very few people do anything single-handed: I was certainly not one of them. The restaurant was originally financed by Irish farming interests, on my suggestion. Peter Robinson, one of the most meticulous and brilliant of the new generation of Irish restaurateurs, got it started in a lovely position at Place du Marché St Honoré. I was taking over from him, redecorating and re-opening it. My son-in-law, Jim, was there to get it going for me. Dominique, our 'French girl', kept the books straight and hostile natives at bay. Jim, the chef, and Rory cooked like two demons at the furnace. Josephine added a touch of Irish beauty which masked a capacity for a lot of Irish hard work. Florence, Jim's wife, quietly did everything else.

The Square is near the Opera and the smart streets. It houses chic little restaurants and superb food shops, yet the atmosphere is that of a village. Two days before we re-opened, I found the neighbours agog with curiosity, popping in and out to see what we were doing. They helpfully offered equipment and advice, such as 'Don't charge too little'. On our opening night, they sent bouquets. A new restaurant in Paris is like a new theatre show.

And so ten days after the bustling morning of departure in Ireland, our doors opened in the quiet, warm, relaxed atmosphere of an August evening in Paris.

If stew went out to Paris, sauces came back.

White Fish Stock

This is needed for several of the following recipes. It is a wonderful colourless flavouring for fish sauces in general, or for using as a clear poaching liquid.

Make sure that there is no speck of blood or fish skin with the bones. Taking out specks of blood will take a little time. When the bones are prepared, put them into a saucepan with the herbs, vegetables, peppercorns, wine and water and simmer for 30 minutes. Strain.

900 g/2 lbs fish bones
300 ml/10 fl oz/½ pt white wine
900 ml/30 fl oz/1½ pts water
85 g/3 oz sliced carrots
85 g/3 oz sliced onions
½ leek
1 celery stick
1 bay-leaf
1 unpeeled clove garlic
sprig of thyme
few parsley stalks
6 black peppercorns

Spinach Butter Sauce

For trout, salmon and bass. Serves approx. 6. Boil cream down to a tablespoonful, or until in danger of burning or turning yellow. Beat in the butter bit by bit, as for Hollandaise sauce. Meanwhile boil about 600 ml/1 pint/2½ cups of water; add salt only if using unsalted butter. Cook spinach leaves in this for 5 minutes. Remove, drain and chop into roughly 2.5 cm/1 in pieces. Stir into sauce. Fish stock can be added to thin this sauce.

225 g/½ lb spinach leaves
250 ml/8 fl oz/1 cup cream
140 g/5oz/10 tablesp. butter

Baked Rainbow Trout in Spinach Sauce

Serves approx. 2. Season the fish. Put it with butter and fennel into tin foil. Wrap into a parcel, folding so that no butter can escape during the cooking. Bake approx. 30 minutes at 190°C/375°F/Regulo 5. Unwrap, and place the fish on a heated serving dish. Be careful to catch all the cooking juices and stir them into the Spinach Butter Sauce.

900 g/2 lbs trout
30-55 g/1-2 oz/2-4 tablesp.
   butter
salt and pepper
sprig of fennel
Spinach Butter Sauce
tin foil

Salmon with Cucumber Hollandaise Sauce

Serves approx. 6. Poach salmon. Finely dice cucumber and cook as described on page 109, using a little snipped fennel leaf instead of mint. Stir the cucumber into the Hollandaise sauce, adding as much juice as is required to make the sauce light.

1.35-1.8 k/3-4 lbs salmon
Hollandaise sauce
½ cucumber
butter
fennel sprig

53

Monkfish

Twenty years ago, nobody touched monkfish around here. I suppose the ugly face and body put everybody off trying the delicious tail. It lives on the sea bed about 3 miles off Ballycotton.

The texture of fresh monkfish is much like lobster or prawns, but without their distinctive flavour.

To prepare monkfish, cut the tail into two fillets off the bone. Carefully cut away all the thin grey skin and membrane that surrounds it, leaving only the white flesh. This can be cut into fingers like prawn-tails for frying in batter or into 1.25 cm/½ in thick slices for poaching in salted water or fish stock. It can then be served with a homely cheese sauce, or herb butter, or a sophisticated White Monkfish Sauce or Red Pepper Sauce.

The Red Wine Sauce on the opposite page makes a surprising and delicious sauce for a simple poached fish such as cod or ling. Use also with fillets of sole, plaice or turbot poached in white fish stock.

Red Wine Sauce

For sole, plaice, brill or turbot fillets. Boil wine, vinegar and shallots together until reduced to 2 tablespoons. Beat in butter bit by bit, as for Sauce Beurre Blanc. Boil down 600 ml/1 pt/2½ cups of fish stock to 150 ml/¼ pt/⅝ cup. Add it to the Beurre Rouge, tasting and using your discretion as to how much you put in. It will greatly improve the flavour of the sauce.

Note: Red Wine Sauce starts with making a Beurre Rouge. The only difference between Beurre Rouge and Beurre Blanc is the colour of the wine and vinegar.

300 ml//½ pt/10 fl oz red wine, of a good colour
60 ml/2 fl oz/¼ cup red wine vinegar
1 shallot finely chopped or diced
170/6 oz/¾ cup butter
white fish stock

White Monkfish Sauce

Take fish stock, made as above. Reserve some for poaching the fish. Reduce 600 ml/1 pt/2½ cups down to 2 or 3 tablespoons. Stir into the Sauce Beurre Blanc. Keep at about blood heat until ready to serve.

White Fish Stock
Sauce Beurre Blanc

Red Pepper Sauce

For monkfish. Serves approx. 6. Dice pepper flesh into 3 mm/⅛ in cubes. Sweat gently in a teaspoonful of butter in a covered pot until soft. Boil down cream and add butter as for Spinach Sauce, finally stirring in the red pepper. Green peppers can be used successfully instead of red.

1 red pepper
250 ml/8 fl oz/1 cup cream
140 g/5 oz/10 tablesp. butter

Freshness

The thing that matters most about fish is its freshness. The extreme urgency of getting fish from the sea to table is not properly appreciated. I can't see why anybody living within 200 miles of the coast should have to eat fish that is more than 36 hours out of the sea, since we no longer depend on horse transport. Refrigeration is no help, if only used for holding fish in storage longer.

It would be a good idea if fish could be time and date labelled as they were caught, automatically dropping 10% of their value every 12 hours. It would then be better business for the fish dealers to sell quickly, though canning and freezing a surplus is quite a different matter.

Plaice Recipes

Any flat fish fillet can be used instead of plaice. I use mainly plaice because it is caught in abundance in Ballycotton Bay. The flavour is delicious when freshly caught from a small boat with a small trawl. It is much more disappointing when taken from a big trawler as it gets bruised in the big catch. Extremely simple cooking is appropriate to fully appreciate the flavour.

The staler the fish, the more trouble the cook must take. There are compensations, however. The recipes can be made in advance, piped with pommes duchesse and refrigerated until needed.

Plaice fillets can be stuffed or sandwiched with any of the creamy shellfish mixtures, topped with buttered crumbs, and baked until cooked through and brown on top.

Fillets of Plaice à la Meunière

Take a heavy iron frying pan. Melt barely enough butter in it to cover the bottom of the pan. Dip the plaice in seasoned flour and cook to a light brown on both sides. Too much butter will delay browning, but one usually needs to add a little more when the fish is turned. Very careful control of the heat is necessary for a perfect finish. When cooked, remove fillets to a hot serving dish. Heat more butter in the pan, squeeze in some lemon juice at the foaming stage and pour it over the fillets. Serve immediately.

Allow per person:
225 g/½ lb fish fillets
30 g/1 oz/2 tablesp. butter
lemon juice
seasoned flour

Plaice in Herb Butter

Wash the fish and clean the slit very thoroughly. With a very sharp knife, cut through the skin, right round the fish, 1.25 cm/½ in from the edge. Be careful to cut right through and to join the side cuts at the tail or you will be in trouble later on. Sprinkle the fish with salt and pepper and lay it in 7 mm/¼ in water in a shallow baking tin. Bake in a moderately-hot oven, 200°C/400°F/Regulo 6, for 20-30 minutes according to the size of the fish. The water should have just evaporated as the fish is cooked. Meanwhile melt the butter and stir in the herbs. Just before serving, pull off the skin (it will tear badly if not properly cut), and spoon over the butter.

To fillet plaice: Clean the fish. Make an incision down the centre back from head to tail with a very sharp knife. Slip the knife under the flesh and cut away from the bone, starting from the centre back with the left-hand fillet first.

To skin the fillets: Place fillet skin-side down on a rough table or chopping board. With knife held at a 45° angle to the fish, cut flesh away from skin with a sawing movement. Start from tail end first.

Allow per person:
1 plaice
15-30 g/½-1 oz/1-2 tablesp. butter
1 teasp. mixed finely-chopped parsley, chives, fennel, thyme leaves

In Ballycotton

In Ballycotton on a calm summer evening the pier is packed with buyers. The commercial men with vans, the hoteliers and just ordinary people hoping for something for their supper.

The fishermen have already taken the precaution of nailing their silver treasures into wooden boxes at sea. One man stands by the pier beside a placid donkey and a cart. The crowd press around. He is the only person who can rescue some of the catch from its long journey and give it to the customer in prime condition. He will set out with some more fish for the townspeople of Cloyne. He just stands at the cross and the word goes round in a flash. Very soon the cart is empty and the little donkey has a lighter load to carry home to Ballycotton. His master, Tommy Sliney, has spent no money on refrigeration. His energy is concentrated on getting the fish straight from the boats to the people — a good man, a fair price and fresh fish.

Batter

'Scampi' and batter-fried fish fillets have been so commercialised, people have forgotten how really good they can be if the batter is crisp, the fillets are fresh, and the frying fat is a sweet fresh dripping or a very good oil. The mixing and beating must be very thorough during making, or the batter will disintegrate when it is put into hot fat — it will fly off the fish in a thousand splinters. If this happens, put the batter into a saucepan, warm it up to about blood heat. If it starts to thicken and go lumpy, remove from heat and beat vigorously until smooth. This treatment binds the batter together again. It is essential to have some fat in batter to give a crisp texture. Cream, butter or oil can be used.

Sweet Batter: Add $\frac{1}{2}$ tablespoon castor sugar to the flour before mixing.

Plaice with Cheese and Mushrooms

6 whole plaice
aromatic herbs and vegetables
4 or 5 peppercorns
340 g/$\frac{3}{4}$ lb sliced mushrooms
7$\frac{1}{2}$ g/$\frac{1}{4}$ oz/$\frac{1}{2}$ tablesp. butter
250-500 ml/8-16 fl oz/1-2 cups creamy milk
roux
170 g/6 oz/1$\frac{1}{2}$ cups grated cheese
1 egg yolk
1 tablesp. cream

Serves approx. 6. Have plaice filleted. Put bones, head and skins of fish in saucepan with herbs and vegetables. Barely cover with cold water, to make a court bouillon. Simmer for 20 minutes. Strain. Fold fillets, place in flat baking dish and cover with court bouillon. Bake for 15 minutes or simmer on top of cooker for 10 minutes. Season mushrooms and cook lightly in a nut of butter. Thicken any pan liquid left after cooking. Place this on the bottom of an oven-proof serving dish. Lay fillets on top. Measure fish cooking water and make up to 750 ml/1$\frac{1}{4}$ pt/3 cups with milk. Thicken with roux. Boil up and finally add 250 ml/8fl oz/1 cup grated cheese and the yolk mixed with cream. Spoon this sauce over the fillets, sprinkle with remaining cheese and heat until brown at the top of a hot oven.

Batter for Fish Fillets

To coat approx. 900 g/2 lbs fish. Serves approx. 4. Sift flour and salt into a bowl and make a hollow in the middle. Put egg and melted butter or cream and a little milk in the hollow and stir, gradually drawing in the flour from the sides. Keep adding milk to the centre. When all the flour is drawn in, beat very thoroughly with a whisk or wooden spoon, or put in a blender at high speed for 30 seconds. Add sufficient milk until the mixture will coat the back of a spoon. It will thicken a little if left to stand. It will keep a day or two in a fridge.

70 g/2 ½ oz/½ cup flour
large pinch of salt
120 ml/4 fl oz/½ cup fresh or
*   sour cream*
*   or*
1 tablesp. melted butter
½ egg
*   or*
1 egg white
175 ml/6 fl oz/¾ cup milk
*   approx.*

Never drown a fresh fish.

Poached Fish

One of the worst aspects of turning one's home into a restaurant is when one arrives back tired after a day out, invariably to face a crisis at the moment when one least wants one.

On one such occasion, everything seemed perfectly under control. My sweetest of students offered to bring me some supper by the sitting-room fire. I chose the fresh fish of the evening, poached with Hollandaise sauce. After one bite, I shot out of my seat; the crisis was on after all. What did he mean, selling us stale fish? It tasted really old. Would I run first to the kitchen or the phone? I ran to the kitchen. Ah! There was the trouble, one small mullet lying in a large preserving pan of water. That was what was wrong with the fish. The instructions below were speedily given to the now rather dismayed student and another fish was prepared before more orders came in from the dining-room. This is important as it would only take about 600 ml/1 pt/2½ cups water to cover a large fish instead of perhaps 2.25 l/4 pts/10 cups. This makes a big difference to its flavour.

Use Salmon, Mackerel, Pollock, Cod, Haddock, Hake, Bass, Grey Mullet, or any round fish. It must be very fresh. Choose a saucepan or fish kettle which will hold the fish tightly. If you cut off the head and tail and halve the fish, you can pack it tightly into a much smaller saucepan. Cover with boiling salted water, allowing 1 teaspoon salt to 600 ml/1 pt/2½ cups water. Simmer for approx. 10 minutes per 450 g/1 lb. Test by inserting a knife as far as the bone in the middle of the thickest part. The flesh should lift off the bone easily. Keep fish in cooking water until ready to serve. Remove fish to a large dish. Fillet and skin it and arrange fillets on a heated serving dish. Coat them with Herb Butter, Hollandaise or Herbed Hollandaise, Beurre Blanc or Garlic Mayonnaise. The cooking water is very good for fish soup.

Baked Fish

Baking is also for very fresh fish. Sprinkle the fish with salt and pepper. Dab on butter. Wrap in foil.

A 1.8k/4 lb fish bakes in about 30 minutes at 190°C/375°F/Regulo 5.

Fish Baked in Crumbs

fillets of any round fish
cheese sauce
buttered crumbs
grated cheese
garlic (optional)
chopped parsley (optional)

Lay fillets skin-side down on a greased baking dish. Top with cheese sauce, sprinkle with buttered crumbs and grated cheese. Garlic and parsley may be added to the sauce. Bake in a moderate oven; time depends on the thickness of the fillets: 15-30 minutes approx.

Fish Baked in Cream

Good for any round fish. Take a frying pan that holds exactly the amount of fish you wish to cook. Melt butter. Fry onions in it for 2 minutes. Add fish and brown on both sides. Add bay-leaf and seasoning. Cover and bake in a moderately-hot oven for 10 minutes approx., when fish should be cooked through. Remove bay-leaf, thicken with roux and taste for seasoning. Add enrichment.

Allow per person:
2.5 cm/1 in thick chunk of cod
* without skin or bone*
1 teasp. chopped onion
½ teasp. butter
120 ml/4 fl oz/½ cup creamy milk
small scrap of bay-leaf
salt and pepper
* roux*

Enrichment:
2 teasp. Hollandaise or Béarnaise
* sauce*
* or*
piece of butter
* or*
very thick cream

A Mixed Fish Fry (sounds like a transport café)

The Italians have a better term, 'Fritto Misto di Mare', which is positively romantic. So much depends on a name, particularly if you want to sell it in a restaurant.

I usually serve a mixture of shellfish and fillets of flat fish fried in different ways, i.e. à la meunière, in egg and crumbs or in batter. With them go stuffed mussels and tiny deep-fried croquettes of the dressed crab mixture in egg and crumbs or the Dutch Cheese Croquettes. Serve with two sauces: Mâitre d'Hôtel or Garlic Butter, Tartare Sauce or Garlic Mayonnaise. Decorate your dish with bunches of parsley and wedges of lemon.

A Sea Food Hollandaise

Same idea. All the fish is carefully poached and served together with a coating of Hollandaise Sauce. Do not poach the fish in the same water. You do not want to get the flavours mixed at this stage.

Rory

When my son Rory was small, the fishermen would sometimes take him out to sea. For their lunch, they would boil freshly-caught mackerel in salt water. One day Rory caught a salmon in a lake in Kerry. I cooked some most carefully. He was very pleased and said it was nearly as good as trawlermen's mackerel. One must accept compliments as they come!

Baked Stuffed Mackerel

Allow per person:
1 mackerel
7½ g/¼ oz/½ tablesp. butter
seasoned flour
2 tablesp. chopped mushrooms
2 teasp. chopped herbs
garlic
salt and pepper

Wash and clean fish very carefully. Melt butter. Soften onions in it. Stir in crumbs and herbs. Pack this mixture into the slit and tie up with string. Season fish and place on a greased baking dish. Bake in a moderately-hot oven, 200°C/400°F/Regulo 6, for 20-30 minutes.

Sauté of Mackerel with Mushrooms and Herbs

Allow per person:
1 mackerel
7½ g/¼ oz/½ tablesp. butter
seasoned flour
2 tablesp. chopped mushrooms
2 teasp. chopped herbs
garlic
salt and pepper

De-bone the fish. Dip the fillets in seasoned flour and fry in hot butter. When nearly cooked, add the mushrooms, herbs, garlic and a little salt to taste. Serve this garnish in a line down the centre of each fillet.

Fish Cakes

Mix together. Roll into balls or fingers. Dip in seasoned flour, egg or egg white and bread crumbs. Deep fry.

225 g/½ lb cold left-over fish
110 g/¼ lb mashed potatoes
1 egg yolk
30 g/1 oz/2 tablesp. butter
salt and pepper

Fish Pie

Layers of cooked flaked fish sprinkled with raw finely chopped onion, chopped parsley, hard boiled egg. Mashed potato top and between layers to spin it out. Bind with white sauce or cheese sauce.

It is easier to take fish off the bone while it is still hot.

Maître d'Hôtel Butter

Soften the butter and stir in the parsley and lemon juice. Roll into pats or wrap in a butter-wrapper, screwing each end so that it looks like a cracker. Refrigerate to harden. Unwrap and cut into rounds.

Allow per person:
15 g/½ oz/1 tablesp. butter
   approx.
1 teasp. finely-chopped parsley
few drops of lemon juice

Grilling Fresh Fish

Fish under 900 g/2 lbs, such as mackerel, herring and brown trout, can be grilled whole on the pan. Fish over 900 g/2 lbs can be cut off the bone into two large fillets. Fish over 1.8 kg/4 lbs can be filleted first and then cut across into portions. Large fish, 1.8-2.7 kg/4-6 lbs, can also be grilled whole. Cook them for 10-15 minutes approx. on each side and then put in a hot oven for another 15 minutes or so to finish cooking.

Heat the grill pan. Dip the fish into flour seasoned with salt and pepper. Spread a little butter on one side, about as much as you would put on a slice of bread. Put the fish, butter side down, diagonally across the hot dry grill. To make the authentic criss-cross mark of the grill, lift the fish after about 4 minutes of cooking, and turn it to face the other direction. Do not move it again, until it is time to turn it over to grill on the other side. Finish cooking and serve with the side that was cooked first uppermost.

To test if a whole fish is cooked, press in the centre of the thickest part. It should be soft right through to the bone. Do not overcook. Serve with a Maître d'Hôtel Butter.

Allow per person:
340 g/¾ lb fish
seasoned flour
butter

Fish at Istanbul

Istanbul is set on rounded hills. Each steep street leads down to a shining arm of the sea, the Bosporus, the Golden Horn and the Sea of Marmara. Every evening, the fishing boats come in, right up to the quays in the centre of the city.

The quality of the fish is not wonderful by our standards, but what a delicious smell wafts up from the boat tied to the quay beside the bus terminus. The crew fry their catch in oil on a stove on deck and sell it in paper wrappings to the people waiting for the buses.

Fish is also cooked and sold from stalls with braziers near the Galata Bridge. Underneath the bridge, little restaurants on pontoons sell every kind of fish they can get, with Turkish wine and fruit and other things.

On the quay at the other side of the bridge, the boats sell the fish raw to the women who want to take it home to cook themselves.

Later, in the evening, round by the beach under the Sultan's Palace, more expensive restaurants are crowded and convivial and their biggest trade is still this rather poor-quality fish — delicious because it is so fresh.

Our whiting and pollock are just as good as their fish. Cod, hake, and ling are much better. I grill them using a method I was taught in one of the very good restaurants, south of Lyon. It makes them as good as Istanbul fish.

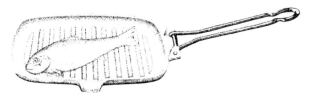

Place diagonally across a grill pan. Cook for 5-7 minutes.

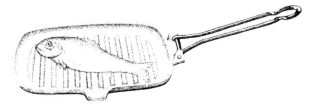

Turn to lie diagonally across the pan in the other direction.

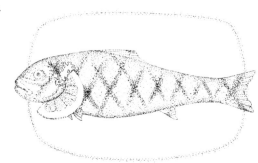

When cooked, the fish will be decorated with a trellis of grill marks.

Pollock for the Party

It's a funny business, the restaurant trade. Turkey sells well from April to October. Coming up to Christmas and for three months after, I can't sell any. Irish stew sells to a French or American clientele, but never to English or Irish. The same goes for my Sauté of Calves Liver. As soon as Christmas is over, everyone wants fresh fish and steaks, regardless of nationality.

One year I was expecting nearly 200 for the New Year's Eve party. The only fish caught was pollock. I had to find some way of getting it out fast, in large quantities, and it had to be delicious. Up to about an hour before dinner I still didn't know what to do. I could feel the tension rise amongst the chefs for fear my brain would fail me and we'd all end up in a panic. They urged me to drop the fish course. In the end, I solved the problem and produced the recipe below.

This dish is designed to serve a number of people at once. Everything is prepared in advance, but the dish is assembled at the last minute. It takes some care and some skill in the saucing.

Party Pollock

Serves approx. 20. Have pollock filleted and skinned. Simmer milk with bouquet garni, garlic, peppercorns, carrot and onion for 20 minutes. Strain and thicken to coating consistency with roux. Beat in butter. Season to taste. Put in a bain-marie to keep warm until service.

Toss crumbs in butter and oil over a medium heat. Continue to cook, tossing constantly, until nicely browned. Keep warm. Make up the Hollandaise sauce. Find a place to keep it cool enough not to curdle, and warm enough not to allow it to cool and harden.

Shortly before service cook the pollock fillets à la meunière — that is to say, dipped in seasoned flour and fried in *very* little butter until crisp and brown on both sides and cooked through. Keep warm until needed — say up to 15 minutes approx.

When the dish is needed, transfer the pollock onto serving plates and carefully coat with a thin film of white sauce. Coat again with a thin film of Hollandaise sauce. Cover with a final coating of crumbs. If done properly, one gets the delicious crisp top covering two distinct layers, golden and white, with the fish underneath. If the sauce is too thick or all over the plate, the dish loses its distinction and is over-rich.

Note: A bain-marie is a vessel containing hot water, into which you put the saucepan of hot white sauce to keep warm.

3.4 kg/8 lbs pollock fillets approx.
1.2 1/2 pts/5 cups milk
bouquet garni
1 onion, sliced
1 carrot, sliced
2 cloves garlic
20 black peppercorns
salt and pepper
roux
225 g/½ lb/1 cup butter
500 g approx./1¾-2lbs/8 cups soft breadcrumbs
butter and oil
Hollandaise sauce
seasoned flour

Poultry

TIM ALLEN

Chickens and Turkeys – Quantities

Chicken and Turkey recipes are virtually interchangeable. I do not give party quantities for chickens or small quantities for turkeys. You could choose your bird to suit your numbers. Reckon 3-5 helpings to a chicken and 1 helping per 340 g/¾ lb of turkey.

If ever you find yourself with too big a turkey, you can just saw it in half vertically and freeze or refrigerate one half until needed. A half turkey cooks quicker and can be better than a full one.

½ turkey = 2-3 chickens.

To Increase Quantities: Substitute 1¼ l/quarts for cups, as in the soups, and multiply other ingredients by five. If you wish, use a turkey instead of a chicken.

To Decrease Quantities: Use a chicken instead of a turkey and divide all measures by five. This will reduce the turkey recipes to family-sized proportions.

Roasting Chickens

There are three kinds of chickens on my horizon — free-range roasting chickens; intensively reared, frozen, broiler chickens; and old hens. They all have their uses as far as I'm concerned.

The finest bird is, of course, the free-range roaster. They are not easy to come by. It is everybody's treasure hunt to find a source of supply. Go to the best poultry supplier you can find, explain what you want, and if you can, place a regular order. As a last resort you can rear your own.

This bird makes the kind of old-fashioned Sunday dinner that your grandmother might have served at the beginning of the century. Prepare all the trimmings — a buttery fresh-herb stuffing, creamy bread sauce, or Cumberland sauce, hot boiled or crisp rolled bacon. I always serve homemade sausages and black puddings and colcannon as well. Don't attempt this with a broiler. All your work will be wasted on the tasteless flesh.

Broiler Chickens

Intensively reared, broiler chickens deep fry or sauté well, as their name implies. They are also good baked in a casserole with herbs, vegetables or spices.

Herbs for Chickens and Turkeys

Savoury, parsley, thyme, chives, marjoram, chervil, tarragon.

Vegetables

Celery, carrots, onions, white turnips, leeks.

The Casserole

If possible, use an oval, cast-iron pot just big enough to take the chicken.

Old-Fashioned Roast Chicken

Allow approx. 1 serving per 340 g/³⁄₄ lb chicken. First make a chicken stock by covering the neck, giblets, vegetables and herbs with cold water. Bring to the boil and simmer while the chicken is being prepared and cooked.

Next make the herb stuffing as described below.

If necessary, wash and dry the cavity of the bird, then season and half fill with stuffing. Season the breast and smear with a little butter. Roast in a little good quality dripping, 200°C/400°F/Regulo 6, for 20 minutes approx., reducing heat to 180°C/350°F/Regulo 4 for 45 minutes more approx. The chicken is done when the juices run clear. Prick in the thickest part — between thigh and body.

To make gravy

Spoon off surplus fat from the roasting pan. De-glaze pan juices with stock from the giblets, stirring and scraping well to dissolve meaty deposits. Boil up well and serve in a hot gravy boat.

1.5-2.3 kg/3¹⁄₂-5 lbs free-range roasting chicken with neck and giblets
¹⁄₂ carrot, sliced
¹⁄₂ onion, sliced
bouquet garni
30 g/1 oz/2 tablesp. dripping
7¹⁄₂ g/¹⁄₄ oz/¹⁄₂ tablesp. butter
salt and pepper

Fresh Herb Stuffing

Sweat onions gently in the butter. When beginning to soften, stir in the crumbs, herbs and a little salt and pepper to taste.

45 g/1¹⁄₂ oz/3 tablesp. butter
85 g/3 oz/³⁄₄ cup chopped onion
150 g approx/5-6 oz/1¹⁄₂ cups soft breadcrumbs
2 tablesp. chopped herbs (parsley, thyme, chives, marjoram, savoury)
salt and pepper

Chicken Baked with Butter and Fresh Herbs

Serves 3-4. Season the cavity of the chicken and stuff it with a few sprigs of fresh herbs. Smear the breast with some of the butter. Lay on its side in a casserole. Bake for 20 minutes in a moderately-hot oven, 190°C/375°F/Regulo 5. Remove, turn on the other side and finish cooking.

To make the sauce, remove the surplus fat from the casserole, stir in stock and white wine. Boil well, add 3 or 4 teaspoons of chopped fresh herbs and at the last minute swirl in remaining butter.

1 kg/2¹⁄₂ lbs chicken
45 g/1¹⁄₂ oz/3 tablesp. butter
250 ml/8 fl oz/1 cup chicken stock (made from neck and giblets or bouillon cube)
salt and pepper
250 ml/8 fl oz/1 cup white wine
herbs as above

Chicken Baked with Butter and Leeks

1 teasp. each oil and butter
1 kg/2½ lbs chicken
140 g/5 oz/1½ cups sliced leeks
30g/1 oz/2 tablesp. butter
1 level tablesp. flour approx.
1 egg yolk
250 ml/8 fl oz/1 cup light cream
120-250 ml/4-8 fl oz/½-1 cup
   chicken stock
salt and pepper

Serves 3-4. Season cavity; brown the breast in a little butter and oil in the casserole. Remove the chicken, wipe out casserole and heat remaining butter. Add leeks. Cook them for 2-3 minutes and then put chicken in to cook. Cover and transfer to moderate oven, 190°C/375°F/Regulo 5, for 40 minutes to 1 hour. Remove the chicken when cooked. Sprinkle a little flour into the casserole to absorb any remaining fat. Stir over heat until the flour cooks. Add stock. Beat egg yolk into cream. Add to sauce. Add more stock or cream if too thick. Adjust seasoning. Carve chicken and coat with the sauce.

Serving note: The dish can be put aside at this stage and reheated when required.

Chicken Gruyère

1 chicken

For stuffing:
110 g/4 oz/1 cup sliced onions
15 g/½ oz/1 tablesp. butter
2 teasp. finely-chopped marjoram
pinch of chopped rosemary
French mustard
110 g/4 oz Gruyère cheese
   approx.

For stock:
½ onion
½ carrot
parsley stalks
thyme
½ bay-leaf
water to cover

To finish:
1 teasp. each oil and butter
bouquet of thyme, bay-leaf and
   marjoram
150 ml/5 fl oz/⅝ cup cream
salt and pepper

Serves approx. 4. In a casserole, cook the onion in half the butter until soft and golden. Remove from the heat and season. Keep aside on a spare plate.

Cut off from the chicken carcase the legs and breasts with wings attached. Remove the leg and wing bones. Put the bones and carcase in a saucepan just big enough to hold them. Add a few slices of onion, carrot and herbs for stock. Cover with cold water and simmer, while you prepare the rest of the dish.

Cut a pocket into the breast meat. Spread French mustard inside the leg and into the pocket in the breast. Put in prepared onion, a sprinkling of herbs and a slice of cheese. Roll up the joints and tie with string. Melt the remaining butter with oil in a casserole. Put in the chicken joints and brown all over. If the pot is burned, remove the chicken, wipe it out, put in fresh butter and return chicken joints. Add any remaining onions and bouquet of herbs. Cover with a tight-fitting lid and cook at 190°C/375°F/Regulo 5, for 40-45 minutes until chicken is cooked through. Put the joints on a serving dish, removing string. Spoon around the onions. Strain the stock from the chicken carcase and add 250 ml/8 fl oz/1 cup of this to the casserole, from which surplus fat should be removed. Boil up well and then stir in the cream. Taste and add seasoning if necessary. Pour this over the serving dish and sprinkle with more herbs.

Note: The dish can be refrigerated at this stage and served later. In this case it is a good idea to slice the joints into 1.25 cm/½ in thick rounds, before reheating in the sauce.

Chicken with Turmeric

Season chicken and brown the breast in a little butter and oil in the casserole. Remove and cook oinions in remaining butter in the casserole for a few minutes. Add chicken back. Peel tomatoes. Season with salt, pepper and sugar. Add them also to the casserole with 1 teaspoon of turmeric and crushed clove of garlic. Cover casserole and cook in a moderate oven, 190°C/375°F/Regulo 5, for 40 minutes approx. or until done.

1 teasp. each oil and butter
1 kg/2½ lbs chicken
15 g/½ oz/1 tablesp. butter
110 g/4 oz/1 cup chopped onion
3 medium tomatoes
salt and pepper
½ teasp. sugar
1 teasp. ground turmeric
1 large clove garlic

Rice: Sweat onions in butter. Add turmeric and rice. Fry for a few minutes. Cover with 470 ml/16 fl oz/2 cups stock or water, and add 1 level teaspoon salt. Bring to the boil. Cover and put in the oven for 15 minutes.

15 g/½ oz/1 tablesp. butter
1 tablesp. finely-chopped onion
1 teasp. turmeric
250 ml/8 fl oz/1 cup rice
500 ml/16 fl oz/2 cups stock
   or
   water
1 level teasp. salt

To finish dish: Remove chicken to a warm dish. Degrease juices in casserole and thicken with roux. Carve the chicken and serve the joints in the centre of a hot dish, coated with sauce and surrounded with the rice. This dish can also be put aside — carved and sauced — for reheating later, but the rice should be cooked last.

Cooking Old Hens

The best kind are those that have laid for one season in a deep-litter house. They are often very fat and full of flavour.

Cook them in a heavy iron saucepan with a good lid, in 5 cm/2 in water, some herbs and root vegetables. Various flavours can be introduced at this stage, such as wine, leeks, tarragon, or spices.

Bring to the boil and then transfer to a moderate oven, 180°C/350°F/Regulo 4. Cook for 2-4 hours. Watch that they do not boil dry. The cooking water should by then be deliciously rich, but rather fatty. It should be de-greased, and thickened. It can be used as the basis of a more elaborate sauce or just as it is with chopped parsley added.

Poularde à la Château Marie

Some neighbours cleared some very fine fowl of this kind from their farm at Castlemary. I served them in the restaurant in a Sauce Suprème and called the dish Poularde à la Château Marie. Well, I couldn't call it Castlemary Hen!

De-greasing Cooking Juices

The quickest way is to use a creamer. These are big flat bowls in which milk was left standing in dairies long ago. After 24 hours all the cream had risen to the top. Skimmed milk was then poured off from the bottom of the pan, through a lip fitted with a guard which held back the cream. It works much more quickly for a fatty stock which rises in about 2 minutes. These now have to be specially made to order.

Chicken Pie

Serves approx. 8. Cook fowl as described opposite. Lightly fry mushrooms and sweat onions in butter until soft. Cut bacon into cubes. Remove fowl from pot when ready, carve flesh and de-grease cooking liquid. Arrange sliced chicken in deep pie dish, covering each layer with bacon, onions and mushrooms.

To make sauce
Thicken 600 ml/1 pt/2½ cups cooking liquid and white wine with roux. Boil and stir until smooth and thick. Add cream. Season to taste. Boil up again, pour this over pie and cover with paste. Refrigerate until required. Heat through and brown top in oven.

1 large boiling fowl, 2.3 kg/5 lbs approx.
bouquet garni
450 g/1 lb streaky bacon, cooked
12 button onions
12 button mushrooms
110 g/4 oz/⅞ cup flour
110 g/4 oz/½ cup butter
or
225 g/8 oz/1 cup roux
225 g/½ lb puff pastry
150 ml/5 fl oz/⅔ cup dry white wine
250 ml/8 fl oz/1 cup cream
salt and pepper

Chicken and Bacon Press

Serves approx. 8. Cook hen as described. At the same time boil the bacon in the same pot. When both are cooked and still hot, carve them and put in layers in a meat press or in a bowl with a weighted lid. Leave 24 hours to cool before carving.

1 large boiling fowl
900 g/2 lbs bacon

Poularde à la Château Marie

Serves 6-8. Cook fowl as described opposite. De-grease the cooking liquid. Measure it. Put it in a saucepan, thicken it with roux and beat in cream and egg yolk. Carve the fowl, coat with sauce and surround with Pilaf Rice.
   Rice: Follow recipe as in Chicken with Turmeric but omit the turmeric.
   Note: A much less strong stock will do the pilaf. Carve the chicken first (and keep it warm). Put the carcase back immediately with a little cold water to simmer while you make the sauce. The neck and giblets should also be used to yield their flavour to a stock for the rice.

1 tablesp. finely-chopped onion or shallot
1 tablesp. oil
250 ml/8 fl oz/1 cup rice
500 ml/16 fl oz/2 cups chicken stock
salt and pepper

Buying Ducks

I find it hard to get good results from intensively-reared, frozen ducks. I was once overheard screaming down the telephone to an un-cooperative co-operative manager, 'Do you freeze the ducks before you kill them, then?' Back to the farmer's wife for ducks, or, once again, to an understanding poultry supplier.

A traditional method of cooking the genuine article is hard to beat.

All our ducks are fresh frozen

Roast Duck

Allow approx. 1 serving per 450 g/1 lb of duck. Prepare the stock for gravy. Make the stuffing and roast the duck exactly as for Old Fashioned Roast Chicken. Serve with a lightly-sweetened apple purée.

1 duck

For stock:
neck and giblets
bouquet garni
½ onion, sliced
½ carrot, sliced

For stuffing:
45 g/1½ oz/3 tablesp. butter
85 g/3 oz/¾ cup chopped onion
1 tablesp. freshly-chopped sage
150g approx./5-6 oz/1½ cup soft
  breadcrumbs
salt and pepper
255 g/9 oz/1 cup apple purée

Roast Goose

Allow approx. 1 serving per 450 g/1 lb of goose. Prepare a stock for the gravy. Stuff, season and roast as for Old Fashioned Roast Chicken. Allow 2 hours to cook. Serve with apple purée, as for Roast Duck.

1 goose

For stock:
neck and giblets
bouquet garni
1 onion, sliced
1 carrot, sliced

Goose Stuffing

Boil the potatoes. Peel and slice the apples and onions thinly. Cook them with the herbs in orange juice. Peel the potatoes when cooked and beat them up with the fruit mixture. Add orange rind and seasoning.

Note: Goose and duck stuffings are interchangeable; increase or decrease quantities as required.

900 g/2 lbs potatoes
450 g/1 lb apples
450 g/1 lb onions
2-3 tablesp. orange juice
sprigs of savoury and lemon balm
1 teasp. finely-grated orange rind
salt and pepper
500 g/1 lb 2 oz/2 cups apple purée

Turkey White – Turkey Brown

Another recipe for a young tender turkey. It is rather slow to make in large quantities, but it can be prepared in advance and it looks very pretty on the dish. The white meat is sautéd in butter and served in a sauce of cream and lemon juice, the brown meat served in a dark red wine sauce with herbs, onion, bacon and mushrooms.

The United Hunt Turkey

This recipe is for a more mature bird, of 9-12 months or more. It is cooked like an old hen. Chopped brown meat and a creamy mushroom filling are sandwiched between slices of turkey breast and freshly-boiled ham. They are coated with a sauce made from the turkey cooking water and topped with Béarnaise sauce. It can be made up in advance, and put out quickly in large quantities. The idea developed on such an occasion when I was asked to cater for the local hunt ball. It was after Christmas, the turkeys had grown rather big, and the price had flopped.

If making either of these turkey dishes up in advance, they can be dished complete with piped pommes duchesse, mushrooms a la crème, tomato fondue, or creamed spinach, refrigerated or frozen and re-heated through quickly when required. The texture of the meat deteriorates a little through freezing, however.

Turkey White — Turkey Brown

Serves approx. 30. Cut the breast from the turkey, lay cut-side down on a board and slice across the grain into escallops. Pick the meat from the wings and slice or pound into flat pieces. Do the same with all brown meat. Keep meats separate. Put bones in a saucepan with herbs and vegetables. Barely cover with cold water and leave to simmer while you prepare the rest of the dish.

Dip white meat in seasoned flour and sauté gently in butter until cooked and golden on both sides. Remove from pan. Stir in more butter and then cream, stirring and scraping while it boils. Add more cream as it boils down, and a squeeze of lemon juice. Put white meat back in sauce. Season carefully to taste.

Cook mushrooms in a little butter for about one minute. Season them and put aside. clean out pan. Dip the brown meat in seasoned flour. Sauté gently in a little more butter until brown on both sides and cooked. Remove from heat. Cook onions in the pan for 5 minutes to soften. Stir in red wine, scrape pan well and boil up. Add 250 ml/8 fl oz/1 cup stock from turkey bones, cooked onions, mushrooms and chopped herbs. Thicken slightly with roux. Cook together for a few minutes. Put the brown meat back into the sauce. Season carefully to taste.

Arrange white and brown meat in a large flat serving dish divided by Pommes Duchesse, Tomato Fondue and Creamed Spinach or other colourful vegetables of your choice.

7 kg/14-15 lbs turkey
For Stock:
1 carrot
1 onion
bouquet garni
For each 450 g/1 lb white meat
  allow:
70 g/2½ oz/½ cup seasoned flour
30-55 g/1-2 oz/2-4 tablesp.
  butter
470 ml/16 fl oz/2 cups cream
lemon juice
For each 450 g/1 lb brown meat
  allow:
70 g/2½ oz/½ cup seasoned flour
110 g/¼ lb/1½ cups sliced
  mushrooms
85 g/3 oz/½ cup approx. chopped
  bacon
250 ml/8 fl oz/1 cup red wine
55 g/2 oz/4 tablesp. butter for
  frying
chopped herbs

The United Hunt Turkey

Serves approx. 30. Boil ham and cook turkey as for an old hen. Make up Mushrooms à la Crème mixture. Make up white sauce. Make up Béarnaise sauce. Remove turkey when cooked. De-grease and thicken cooking liquid. Spread white sauce mixed with some of the Mushrooms à la Crème on the serving dishes, having made sure the seasoning is correct.

Carve a nice slice off the breast for each helping; lay it on the sauce.

Carve brown meat and wing meat, chop it up and mix it with the remainder of the Mushrooms à la Crème. Mix through some chopped parsley and other herbs, and a little French mustard to taste. Put a tablespoon of this mixture on top of turkey breast slices. Carve ham and put a slice on top of the mushroom mixture.

Mix turkey cooking liquid with any remaining white sauce. Beat in some Béarnaise sauce and coat the dish with this. Put a little more Béarnaise sauce on top to brown. Surround with Pommes Duchesse. Refrigerate until required. Reheat and serve immediately.

5.5-6.5 kg/12-14 lbs turkey
3-4.5 kg/7-10 lbs lean ham
Mushrooms à la Crème (made
  from 1 kg/2½ lbs mushrooms)
60 g/2 oz/1 cup chopped parsley
other fresh herbs as available
1.5 l/2½ pts/6¼ cups white sauce
French mustard
450 ml/¾ pt/2 cups scant/
  Béarnaise sauce
225 g/8 oz/1 cup approx. roux

The Most Harassing Problem

The most harassing problem in a restaurant kitchen is that of time. If a customer asks for something, he wants it immediately. Not in half an hour which would be convenient for the cook, who is already in the process of doing something else for several other people, who also want their orders immediately.

One night some important guests sent an order to the kitchen for redcurrant sauce. I hadn't prepared any that night, but assured the waitress that I could make it in a minute from frozen fruit. I rushed to the freezer, a chest type, to get some. The freezer was almost empty, it is deep, and I am short and they were completely stuck to the floor. I literally dived in, legs in the air, but no matter how hard I pulled, I couldn't get out the bag. To break it meant scattering them everywhere.

I imagined them furiously toying with their turkey, and impatiently demanding their sauce. I got redder in the face and my fingers more and more bruised and frozen. I wondered if they realised what it was like to be a restaurateur and not a customer. If they could see me, would they laugh?

A Turkey In Summer

We get the first young turkeys of the season in June. They weigh 3.5-4.5 kg/8-10 lbs and are very fleshy and tender, but at this time of year one does not want to be reminded of Christmas.

I season the breast, cut the skin here and there and insert a paste of butter and fresh herbs. Sprigs of fresh herbs are put in the seasoned cavity and then the bird is casserole roasted like a chicken. I serve it with young peas, carrots, new potatoes, and a sauce of redcurrants which should be ripening about then. Alternatively, later in the summer, it can be cooked with watercress instead of herbs.

Redcurrant Sauce

Boil ingredients together until the fruit is soft. Serve with ham, chicken, guinea fowl, bacon, chops etc.

*110 g/4 oz/1 cup redcurrants
(strings removed)
170 g/6 oz/³/₄ cup sugar
120 ml/4 fl oz/¹/₂ cup water*

Turkey Baked with Butter and Watercress

Serves 10-14. Do not disjoint bird (unless your casserole is too small!). Season and brown the breast of a small turkey in oil and butter in a very large, heavy casserole, then remove it. If the fat burns, throw it out and start again with fresh butter. Sweat onion and garlic in the casserole for 5 minutes and then put in the turkey. Bake 2¹/₂ hours approx. in a moderately hot oven, 190°C/375°F/Regulo 5. Do not let the bottom of the pot burn. Remove turkey to a carving dish.

Press pot juices with a little of the onion through a sieve. Degrease. Sweat watercress, parsley and garlic for the sauce in the butter for about 1 minute to cook very lightly. Stir mixture into pot juices and add cream with seasoning to taste.

*4.5-5.4 kg/10-12 lb turkey
55 g/2 oz/4 tablesp. butter
570 g/1¹/₄ lb/5 cups chopped
onion (onion greens may be
included)
4 crushed cloves garlic*

*For Sauce:
110 g/4 oz/2¹/₂ cups chopped
watercress
2 tablesp. chopped parsley
1 clove garlic
7 g/¹/₂ oz/1 tablesp. butter
150-250 ml/4-8 fl oz/¹/₂-1 cup
cream
salt and pepper*

Meat

TIM ALLEN

Beef

The best cuts of prime beef should be kept mainly for roasting and grilling, to be served with the classic English and French sauces. I like to offer a choice of Béarnaise, Horseradish Sauce, and Garlic Mayonnaise with roast beef, with a tomato fondue and green salad as well.

A cheaper cut can be treated as a sauté and then simmered in its sauce until it is tender. Here are two adaptations of famous dishes and one with a genuinely Dublin flavour.

Cooking time will depend on the quality of the beef. Rump steak would be my first choice.

it's just as delicious without the steak!

Strogonoff Stew

Serves approx. 4. Cut the meat into slices. Heat butter and oil in a casserole. Sear meat in this, Remove. Wipe out pot and add fresh butter. Toss onion in this for a few minutes. Do not allow to burn. Put meat back into casserole and add a little stock, not quite enough to cover meat. Season to taste. Cover with lid and cook gently, preferably in an oven, 180°C/350°F/Regulo 4, until meat is tender, 1-3 hours. Meanwhile, slice the mushrooms, season and cook them for 1 minute in a little butter. When meat is cooked, stir in the mushrooms and sour cream. Check seasoning. Decorate with parsley or watercress sprigs and serve immediately.

1 teasp. each oil and butter
450 g/1 lb lean beef
55 g/2 oz/½ cup thinly-sliced onions
15 g/½ oz/1 tablesp. butter
225 g/8 oz/2½ cups sliced mushrooms
60 ml/2 fl oz/¼ cup sour cream
175 ml/6 fl oz/¾ cup stock
salt and pepper

Pepper Beef Stew

Serves approx. 3. Cut meat into a portion per person, 2 cm/½-1 in thick. Heat oil in a heavy casserole. Crush the peppercorns and press them into the meat. Season with salt and sear for 2 minutes on both sides in hot oil. Wipe out pot. Heat half the butter and sauté onions gently in this for 3 or 4 minutes. Return meat with more peppercorns (if too many are lost), wine, stock, garlic and salt to taste. Cover. Simmer gently until meat is cooked as in previous recipe. Remove meat onto a hot serving dish. Boil down the gravy, enrich with remaining butter and check seasoning again. Serve with sauté potatoes and green salad.

450 g/1 lb lean beef
2 teasp. oil
1 onion, sliced
1 glass dry white wine
250 ml/8 fl oz/1 cup stock
15 g/½ oz/1 tablesp. butter
2 teasp. black peppercorns
1 clove crushed garlic

Steak with Stout

Serves approx. 3. Brown meat in half the butter — do not burn it. Add onions and cook 2-3 minutes more. Add herbs tied with a thread, pour over stout and stock, and season to taste. Top with whole peeled potatoes. Cover closely and cook gently until ready. The juices may be slightly thickened with roux and enriched with remaining butter. Serve surrounded by potatoes, sprinkled with chopped parsley.

60 g/2 oz/4 tablesp. butter
450 g/1 lb lean beef
2 onions, sliced
thyme, sage, parsley, bay-leaf
salt and pepper
480 ml/8 fl oz/1 cup stock
3 potatoes
120 ml/2 fl oz/¼ cup stout
chopped parsley

Cut Your Own Steaks

It is very easy and relatively cheap to cut your own steaks provided you know what to do with all the parts. A 3.2 kg/7 lb sirloin with a good undercut of fillet should yield you about four sirloin steaks weighing about 170 g/6 oz each, three fillet steaks of the same weight, or four or five tournedos steaks weighing approx 110 g/3-4 oz each. In addition to these there will be over 450 g/1 lb of bones for the stock pot, 790 g/1¾ lb flank and over 450 g/1 lb beef suet for suet crust pastry, suet pudding or dripping. A 3.2 kg/7 lb piece further down the loin with less undercut will give you more sirloin steaks and the fillet will be much smaller.

Start by cutting off the flank at the narrow flexible middle part below the meaty 'eye' of the sirloin.

Next, plunge the knife in between the top of the joint and the bone. Cut downwards, pressing the knife against the bone. You will be able to feel your way between flesh and bone and gradually you will be able to turn the knife sideways and cut the piece off horizontally. It is like cutting the meat off an enormous chop. Divide the top piece into four or more steaks according to the size of your piece.

Turn the joint the other way up and cut off the undercut or fillet in exactly the same way. There is a good deal of suet around the fillet which will peel off easily.

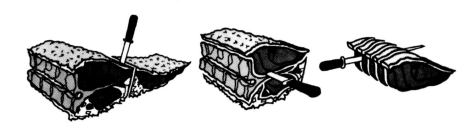

Sprinkle with freshly-ground black pepper, rub with the cut side of a halved clove of garlic; just before grilling, sprinkle with salt and dab with butter. They are best grilled on a heavy cast-iron grill pan heated up before use. Approximate cooking: 3 minutes each side for medium rare; 5 minutes each side for well done.

Fillet Steaks are usually seasoned and grilled in the same way. Beware! A thick fillet will take 20 minutes to cook if it is to be well done. Allow approx. 5 minutes each side for medium rare.

Tournedos Steaks are cut into 2.5 cm/1 in thick slices, trimmed well and tied into neat rounds with thick cotton thread or string. Do not tie them too tightly as they will swell while cooking. Prepare as for sirloins. Serve on a round croûton of fried bread to fit the tournedo. Approx. cooking time: 2 minutes each side for medium rare; 4 minutes each side for well done.

The Flank can be roasted, a little tough sometimes, but of good flavour. It will make any of the stews mentioned, hamburgers, or can be spiced and boiled.

Hamburgers: To 450 g/1 lb of minced flank, add 110 g/4 oz/$\frac{1}{2}$ cup chopped onion previously softened in butter, $\frac{1}{3}$ teaspoon of salt, a few grinds of black pepper, $\frac{1}{2}$ teaspoon of thyme leaves, 1 egg. Mix together well and fry a few crumbs of the mixture before tasting for seasoning. Shape into cakes about 5 cm x 2.5 cm/2 in x 1 in thick, dip in seasoned flour, and cook in a little good fat for 3 minutes approx. on each side. A gravy can be made from the pan juices.

The Old Days

I tremendously admire the smooth organisation of daily life that operated before the motor car and telephone came and enabled us to sail along thoughtlessly until the last minute. There was no rushing out at 12.30 to buy something for lunch in those days.

Life was pre-arranged. If visitors were coming, they had written a week before. My predecessors then sat down and wrote a postcard to the butcher at Cloyne, knowing that he would unfailingly deliver on Friday for the weekend. In summer he would deliver on Tuesdays as well. The meat was fresh; it would not have kept if it had been hung as we now require it. Delicious bread came every day, fresh from the village bakery in Cloyne or Castlemartyr. Eggs, vegetables and butter were sent twice weekly to Bally-cotton from the Ballymaloe Farm in a little donkey cart. The boy who delivered them still works on the farm. Nowadays it is a real treasure hunt to get fresh farm eggs and vegetables in Ballycotton. Milk was delivered to Cloyne every day and twice daily in the summer straight after milking. I don't believe that the milk that now rattles round the roads in a lorry all day is a healthier product.

Of all the arrangements, the only ones that still operate are those of the Cuddigans, the butchers in Cloyne, and the two little bakeries.

The Cuddigans traditionally produced high-quality meat for the gentry of the district. The gentry have gone; their houses are now mostly occupied by families of a different stock. Young Mr Cuddigan, however, continues to run the business the same way. He buys prime heifers and finishes fattening them on the damp lush grass in the flat fields on the south side of Cloyne. His lambs are bought with his meticulous flair for perfection; they must never have received a check in growth from the day they were born. He scorns the cult for lean meat. Once this is understood there is no problem: one hasn't got to eat the fat. I would far prefer to fry in mutton fat than cooking oil anyway.

Beef Cubes

One summer evening I overheard a waitress telling a customer that we had no steaks left. I interrupted the conversation. Yes, we actually had steak meat, but it was all cut into cubes, having been left over from a fondue bour-guignon from the previous night. I would sauté the cubes and serve them in a sauce made with the pan juices. Every fortnight or so for some years after this event, my customer returned and ordered 'Beef Cubes' for her dinner.

Beef Cubes

Cut meat into 1.25 cm/½ in cubes. Heat butter and oil in a frying pan. Toss the meat in this to required degree, about 4 minutes for medium rare. Remove. Cook shallots in pan for 1 or 2 minutes. Pour in wine and then stock. Cook down to half the quantity. Swirl in herbs and a butter enrichment.

Allow per person:
110-225 g/¼-½ lb steak
1 tablesp. white wine
1 teasp. finely-chopped shallots
2 tablesp. stock
1 level teasp. mixed butter and oil
1 teasp. butter
½ teasp. chopped tarragon

Spiced Beef

Below is an old-fashioned recipe for spiced beef. Nowadays, saltpetre is regarded as a health hazard, so perhaps you should not live exclusively on it. Certainly people have lived well on occasional meals of meats preserved in this way for generations. This is one reason why bacon once kept well, though it does no longer.

Spice for approx. 5 flanks. The spices should be well mixed and kept in a jar. Remove the bones from the flank and rub thoroughly with spices. Leave for 2-7 days, turning occasionally. Roll up and tie the joint with string. Put it in a pot, cover with cold water, bring to the boil. Simmer 2-3 hours until soft. If not to be eaten hot, press by putting it on a flat dish with a board on top and a weight on top of that. Leave 12 hours.

250 g/½ lb/1½ cup demerara
  sugar
15 g/½ oz/2 teasp. saltpetre
340 g/12 oz/1 cup salt
85 g/3 oz/generous ½ cup ground
  black pepper
85 g/3 oz/generous ½ cup allspice
85 g/3 oz/1 cup ground juniper
  berries

Tournedos with Mushrooms

Serves 6. Cut bread into rounds to fit tournedos. Fry bacon and shallot together until cooked, 5 minutes approx. Add red wine and stock. Reduce by half and put aside for sauce. Sauté mushrooms in 15 g/½ oz/1 tablesp. butter for a minute. Add them with their juices to the sauce. Fry bread in oil or butter until golden on both sides. Keep warm. Season tournedos and cook in a teaspoon each of hot butter and oil. Place tournedos on top of croutons on a serving dish and keep warm. Pour the reserved sauce into the pan in which they were fried. Boil down to about 120 ml/ 4 fl oz/½ cup liquid, scraping the pan. Stir in the pâté. Pour over steaks and serve immediately. There should not be very much sauce, but it should have thickened and be very full of flavour.

6 tournedos steaks
6 slices bread
butter or oil for frying
55 g/2 oz/⅜ cup diced streaky
  bacon
15 g/2 oz/½ cup finely-chopped
  shallot or spring onion
200 g/7 oz/2 cups sliced button
  mushrooms
250 ml/8 fl oz/1 cup red wine
250 ml/8 fl oz/1 cup stock
15 g/½ oz/1 level tablesp. chicken
  liver pâté

Cloyne Fair

From Norman times up to the 1950s, cattle were mainly bought and sold at fairs. Previously, they were won or lost in raids, wars and marriages. Of course the methods overlapped the dates to a great extent. 1955 brought a decisive change, when the marts were established.

Up to then, a fair was held in Cloyne on the fourth Monday in every month that had five Mondays in it. A fair was held in Fermoy on the first Monday of each month, Midleton on the second, Youghal on the third and Killeagh on the last Monday. These served the farmers of East Cork.

On the night before Cloyne fair the shopkeepers barricaded their windows with wooden planks. From three o'clock onwards the next morning, farmers, their sons and their men were up to drive their fat bullocks, stores and calves, in-calf heifers, milking cows, suckling cows with their calves and any odds and ends of animals they had, along the roads to Cloyne to be sold. Sheep and pigs were sold too, but the main business was in cattle. They stood in groups in the street and on the pavements. The town was packed, the pubs full and what a mess was in the streets when they left in mid afternoon and the shopkeepers ruefully unboarded their glass windows.

The bargaining was an expert job. My husband went in to see how things were going at about 7.30 a.m. He went to Charley Creed's house for a sumptuous gentlemen's breakfast, but he *never* attempted to make a deal. Women never went to the fair at all.

Buying and selling were done for us by Jack Smyth. Jack was noted for his ability to make a good deal. A lifetime of experience had taught him all the tricks of the trade. He knew all the farmers and the dealers. He arranged marriages as well as buying cattle. He would tell a good girl as well as a good heifer and knew what would suit the families. Although marriages were sometimes arranged in the pubs after the fair, they mainly materialised after a long period of negotiation. If Jack Smyth was involved, neither of the partners nor their families would know who was being considered for them up to a late stage in the arrangements. When Jack was going out to negotiate with a family, he drove his pony and trap in the opposite direction to the way he intended to go, so that nobody would guess who he had in mind for the match.

The marriages themselves worked surprisingly well, such was the simplicity of life and the structure and conventions of the times. But, by the 1950s, if the fairs were outdated, the brides had certainly kicked up.

Here are some quickly cooked meat dishes, all products of the cattle trade. The accompanying sauces are cheered up with a little Irish liquor, handy for supper after a fair, perhaps!

Sauté of Calves Liver with Whiskey and Tarragon

Heat butter on a heavy frying pan until it foams. Dip the livers in flour and fry on both sides in the butter. Push the meat to one side of the pan. Pour in the whiskey; if cooking on gas, tilt the pan towards the heat, allowing the flame to leap in to ignite the whiskey. Light with a match otherwise. When the flames have died down, add the stock, garlic and tarragon. Boil down until syrupy. Stir in the cream.

Note: to make concentrated stock, take one cup ordinary household stock and boil down to reduce the volume by half.

Allow per person:
110-170 g/4-6 oz liver slices
seasoned flour
7 g/¼ oz/½ tablesp. butter
1 tablesp. whiskey
120 ml/4 fl oz/½ cup
   concentrated stock
garlic to taste
1 teasp. chopped tarragon leaves
1 tablesp. cream

Shanagarry Porter Steak

Put stock in a saucepan with a bay-leaf and 2 sliced onions. Boil until reduced to a few tablespoons of syrupy liquid. Strain out onion and bay. Fry the steaks on a pan in butter. Just before the steaks are cooked, add the remaining onion (finely chopped) to soften on the pan. Remove the steaks to a warm serving dish and keep warm. Put the reduced stock, 2 tablespoons of stout, and sage into the pan. Boil up and taste. Add more stout, stock, salt and pepper as required. Pour over steaks and serve immediately.

1.2 l/2 pt/5 cups good beef stock
3 onions
6 steaks
1 teasp. butter
2-4 tablesp. porter
½-1 tablesp. finely-chopped sage

Pies and Puddings

Cheaper cuts of beef are also good in a pie or a pudding — steak and kidney, steak and oyster, steak and pigeon. I think it is time that people went back to the pudding. Suet crust is cheap and easy to make, but perhaps it takes a lot of exercise in the cold, fresh air to develop the right sort of metabolism to cope with it.

Cover pies with a good home-made puff, flaky or shortcrust pastry, or the best pastry you can buy.

Plucking Pigeons

Plucking small birds is laborious considering the amount of meat to be got from them. Sometimes it only seems worthwhile to pluck and cut out the breast of the pigeon and throw away the rest of the carcase.

Sunday Pie

You can go surprisingly wild on meat and game pies and still come out on the right side. Occasionally I go into my cold room on a Sunday morning and collect all the left-over pieces of the week — beef, lamb, chicken, bacon, veal, pork, a little bit of liver or kidney, and so on. All get cooked up in the biggest casserole with herbs and vegetables much as for steak and oyster or steak and pigeon pie. They are then transferred to a pie dish, covered with pastry, and baked. So far, it has never failed to be the best pie of all.

If you're broke or you don't have a restaurant-sized meat chill, you can always scrounge scraps from the butcher (pretend it's for the dog!).

Steak and Oyster Pie

12 oysters
680 g/1½ lbs beef
1 onion, chopped
30 g/1 oz/2 tablesp. butter
1 tablesp. flour
170 g/6 oz/2 cups sliced
   mushrooms
600 ml/1 pt/2½ cups stock
salt and pepper
pastry

Serves 4-6. Cut beef into cubes. Season. Heat butter in casserole but do not burn it. Toss first meat and then onions in it, then remove. Stir in flour, cook for a few minutes. Blend in stock, add mushrooms and oysters with their juice. Check seasoning. Put in a pie dish. Cover with pastry and cook for 2 hours in a moderate oven, 180°C/350°F/Regulo 4, or steam in a pudding bowl with suet crust as directed.

Suet Crust for Puddings

Sufficient for a 600 ml/1 pint bowl.

To Prepare Suet: Remove skin and red veins and chop finely or mince.

Mix dry ingredients and moisten to a stiff dough with water. Roll out two thirds dough to about 1 cm/⅜ inch in thickness. Line a china pudding bowl with this. Fill with one of the pie mixtures. Roll remaining dough into a round to fit the top. Moisten edges and stick them together.

Tie a circle of greaseproof paper over the bowl and steam in a saucepan half filled with water for 3 hours — best done in an oven 150°C/350°F/Regulo 4. Turn out onto an oven proof serving dish and return to a hot oven to brown a little before serving.

140 g/5 oz/1 cup flour
200 g approx/7-8 oz/2 cups
*   breadcrumbs*
110 g/4 oz/¾ cup shredded beef
*   suet*
½ teasp. salt
1 level teasp. baking powder

Steak and Pigeon Pie

Serves approx. 8-12. Slice beef and pigeon breasts into strips. Cut rind off bacon and slice in a similar way. Heat a little very good dripping, butter or bacon fat in the bottom of a 1.5 litre/4 pint heavy casserole. Toss the meat, a little at a time, in this until it changes colour. Remove meat from casserole. In it cook carrots and onions in fat for a few minutes. Remove. Be careful all the time that the casserole does not overheat and the fat burn in the bottom. Stir flour into any remaining fat in the casserole. Blend in stock, wine and tomato purée. Thicken with roux if necessary. Return meat and vegetables together with crushed garlic, thyme and parsley. Add mushrooms. Check seasoning. Put in pie dish. Cover with pastry lid and cook for 2-3 hours in a moderate oven, 150°/300°F/Regulo 2-3, or steam in a pudding bowl as directed.

Optional addition: 85 g/3 oz/1 cup of sliced mushrooms or Mushrooms à la Crème.

4-6 pigeon breasts
their weight in lean beef
half their weight in streaky bacon
8 baby carrots or sticks of carrot
fat for frying
1-2 teasp. flour
250 ml/8 fl oz/1 cup red wine
500 ml/16 fl oz/2 cups good
*   stock*
2 teasp. chopped thyme and
*   parsley*
8 button onions
1 clove garlic
150 ml/¼ pt/⅔ cup homemade
*   tomato purée*
*   or*
*   smaller quantity tinned purée*
*   or tomato paste: use according*
*   to concentration and make up*
*   with extra stock*
roux
salt and pepper
pastry

A Late Easter

A late Easter with warm, damp weather upset the man who made our Easter Eggs, as the chocolate was slow to set in the moulds.

An early Easter made my butcher angry. 'The churches really ought to get together and do something about it,' he stormed. This was the proper purpose of ecumenism. He was never known to kill a lamb before Easter, no matter how late it was. The killing of the first lambs and Easter weekend still go together in this district.

If the lamb is ready before my mint bed, it upsets me. It is essential to have one small secret patch in a sheltered place, unknown to my friends, relations and kitchen staff.

Very simple cooking is needed for the first lamb of the season. A chop or noisette can be sautéd gently in butter and mint. Later on, boned and stuffed loin or shoulder is good.

Boning a shoulder is quite difficult, but it is easy to cut the bones away from the loin. Noisettes are 2 cm/½-1 in thick slices cut from the boned loin. Surplus fat is cut out and they are rolled and tied. Sometimes the most difficult part is to find the cotton string to tie the meat.

I'm sorry to tell you this - but when Easter comes, your goose is cooked...

Stuffed Loin of Lamb

Spread stuffing on boned side and roll up and tie like a jam roll. Allow 110-170 g/4-6 oz meat per person. Roast approx. 1½ hours, 180°C/350°F/ Regulo 4.

Stuffing suggestions:
herb stuffing
pork stuffing (use sausage meat)
mixture of cooked or chopped
ham, mushrooms and onions
with buttered crumbs and
chopped mint

Lamb Noisettes in Mint and Butter Sauce

Cut round croûtons of bread of medium thickness the same diameter as the noisettes. Fry them until golden in butter and oil. Keep them warm while you cook the noisettes. Season and sauté the noisettes for 3-4 minutes on each side in foaming butter. Remove from pan. Toss spring onions on pan for 1-2 minutes, add wine and stock, stir and scrape pan while boiling fast. Thicken very slightly with roux and stir in remaining butter and mint. Mount each noisette on a croûton, spoon sauce over and serve immediately.

Allow per serving:
1-2 noisettes
1 heaped teasp. finely-chopped
spring onions
1 tablesp. dry white wine
1 tablesp. stock
1 teasp. roux
butter
1 teasp. mint

Lamb Cutlets in a Casserole

Serves 4. Peel the tomatoes and wipe the mushrooms. Put a layer of tomatoes on the bottom of the casserole, sprinkle with salt, pepper and sugar. Put in a layer of mushrooms, season with salt and pepper. Put chops in and season, add rosemary and garlic and continue in these layers. Top with tomatoes and finally mushrooms. Cover and bake 2 hours in a moderately-hot oven, 180°C/350°F/Regulo 4. De-grease and slightly thicken juices. Serve with mushrooms, tomatoes and chopped parsley scattered on top, juices poured around.

1 kg/2½ lbs neck chops
900 g/2 lbs tomatoes
450 g/1 lb flat mushrooms
small sprig of rosemary
1 clove garlic
roux
salt, pepper, sugar

Stay Out of the Garden, Cook

We used to have a lovely big old rosemary bush in our garden. One cold winter it died. My daughter-in-law, Hazel, who lives in the garden, accused my cooks of picking it to death. They weren't allowed in the garden again for ages. Now I know better, because a friend of mine told me that she lost three mature rosemary bushes in the ravages of that winter.

All the same, cooks are quite insensitive to gardeners' problems and I can't agree with Constance Spry who wrote a book called *Come into the Garden, Cook*. Gardeners also have their limitations. They have no idea how much rosemary, mint, parsley or lettuce is needed by five cooks for ninety dinners.

You might ask, what did my cooks do with so much rosemary, even to be wrongfully accused of taking it all? Well, it would have gone mainly into legs of lamb for roasting, because this is such a nice, easy dish that doesn't ever go wrong. It takes time to prepare, but it is a comfortable way of spending 20 minutes on a kitchen stool. You can chat as you go along and the lamb looks so pretty when it is finished. Here is how to do it. It does not turn out to be too garlicky in flavour.

Lamb Roast with Rosemary and Garlic

Serves approx. 8. With the point of a skewer, make 1 cm/½ in deep holes all over the lamb about 2.5 cm/1 in apart. It is a good idea not to do this on the underside of the joint in case somebody insists on eating their lamb unflavoured.

The rosemary sprigs will divide into tufts of three or four leaves together. Insert a tuft of leaves into each hole.

Peel the garlic cloves and cut them into little spikes about the same size as a matchstick broken into three. Stick a spike of garlic into each hole with rosemary. Leave like this for up to 24 hours.

Heat the oven to 200°C/400°F/Regulo 6. Sprinkle the joint with salt and pepper and put it in the oven. Reduce the heat to 180°C/350°F/Regulo 4 after 20 minutes. Cook approx. 1 hour more for rare lamb, 1½ hours if it is to be well done. Remove the joint to a serving dish. Spoon the fat off the roasting tin. Pour stock into the cooking juices remaining in the tin. Boil for a few minutes, stirring and scraping the pan well. Strain and serve separately in a gravy boat.

2.7 kg/6 lbs leg lamb
4-5 cloves garlic
2 sprigs of rosemary
300 ml/½ pt/1¼ cups stock

Dingle Pies

Pies were made for special occasions in Dingle, for Lady Day in September, Holy Thursday and November's Day (All Saints). They were made for fair days when nobody had time to sit down to a proper meal but the pie shops flourished and the children chattered with delight:

> 'Make a pie, make a pie, make a pie,
> Roll a pie, roll a pie, roll a pie,
> Pinch a pie, pinch a pie, pinch a pie.'

For the farmers and fishermen they provided a sustaining snack. They were made from scraps of mutton or the meat of a sheep's head, for Dingle is in mountainous sheep country. It is a sheltered meeting place before that long, wild peninsula plunges into the great Atlantic.

There were several recipes for mutton pies in and about Dingle. All are very simple. The pastry was shortened with butter, dripping or mutton fat, sometimes moistened with hot milk. It was rolled out and cut with a saucer. The meat was seasoned and heaped in the middle and a smaller circle of pastry, cut with a tumbler, was placed on top. The pastry base was brought up to fit oven the top circle, pleated to fit, the edges moistened and pinched on. They were baked in a slow to moderate over for about an hour, or boiled in a stock made out of the mutton bones. Fishermen brought them to sea in a can and heated them up in the stock over a little fire made in a tin box, at the bottom of the boat. A cold baked pie was better for the farmer's pocket.

The spiced mutton pies opposite are not Dingle Pies, but were inspired by them — a more sophisticated descendant. The pastry is a rich hot water crust, made with a lot of butter. Serve hot or cold. Good for picnics.

Spiced Mutton Pies

For two 16 cm x 6.5 cm/6 in x 1½ in pies, 6-8 helpings.

Put bones and vegetable trimmings in cold water and simmer to make a stock, if none is already available. Cut surplus fat away from the meat. Chop it finely and render it down in a heavy pot over a medium heat. Cut the remaining meat into small neat pieces about the size of sugar lumps. Cut the vegetables into slightly smaller dice and toss them in the fat in the bottom of the pot, leaving them to cook for 3-4 minutes. Remove the vegetables and toss the meat in remaining fat until the colour turns. Stir in flour and spice. Cook gently for 2 minutes and blend in the stock gradually. Bring to the boil, stirring occasionally. Add the vegetables and leave to simmer in a covered pot. If using young lamb, 30 minutes will be sufficient; an older animal can take up to 2 hours. Meanwhile make pastry cases.

450 g/1 lb boneless mutton
275 g/9 oz/2¼ cups onions
275 g/9 oz/1¾ cups carrots
1 teasp. cumin seed
300 ml/10 fl oz/1¼ cups stock
2 tablesp. flour
salt and pepper

Sieve flour and salt into a mixing bowl, and make a well in the middle. Put butter and water into a saucepan and bring to the boil. Pour the liquid all at once into the flour and mix together quickly; beat until smooth. At first the pastry will be too soft to handle, but as it cools it can be rolled out 5 mm/⅛-¼ in thick to fit two tins 15 cm/6 in in diameter, 4 cm/1½ in high. It can also be made into individual pies as described opposite. Keep back one-third of the pastry for lids. Fill up the cases with the meat mixture which should be almost, but not quite, cooked and cooled a little. Moisten the pastry at the top of the pies and place the lids on, pinching them tightly together. Cut a slit in the lid, brush with egg wash. Bake the pies for 40 minutes approx. at 190°C/ 375°F/Regulo 5. They can be eaten hot or cold and are good for picnics.

450 g/1 lb/3½ cups flour
255-285 g/9-10 oz/1¼ cups
  approx. butter
175 ml/6 fl oz/¾ cup water
pinch of salt

Irish Stew

I spent one period of my life going around asking everyone I met, 'Do you put carrots in your Irish Stew?' The answer was invariably, 'Yes'.

My mother always put carrots in her stew, everyone in Shanagarry did too. I found carrots going into the Irish Stew as far north as Tipperary. The classic version has no carrots, but it is common practice to include them in the south, at any rate. As this is a traditional folk dish, I feel that common practice carries its own authenticity.

Originally we made Irish Stew by putting alternate layers of onions, carrots, potatoes and meat in a pot. It was seasoned, covered with water and stewed gently for 2 hours. Very simple and enjoyable.

Later on, when my children were small, a good woman called Madge Dolan came to cook for us and brought us a new and better version, which is the basis of our present recipe.

My whole life has been one great stew after another

Ballymaloe Irish Stew

Serves 4. Shred some of the mutton fat and render it down in a heavy casserole. Peel onions and potatoes, scrape carrots. Cut the meat into 8 pieces; only excess fat is cut away. Bones need not be removed. Cut the carrots and onions in quarters. Toss meat in fat until colour changes and repeat with onions and carrots. Add stock and season carefully. Put whole potatoes on top. Simmer gently until the meat is cooked, 2 hours approx. Pour off the cooking liquid. De-grease and reheat in another saucepan. Check seasoning. Then swirl in butter, chives, parsley and pour back over stew.

1.3 k approx./2½-3 lbs mutton neck chops
4 medium-sized carrots
4 medium-sized onions
15 g/½ oz/1 tablesp. butter
mutton fat or good dripping
salt and pepper
600 ml/1 pt/2½ cups stock or water
4 potatoes
1 tablesp. chopped parsley
1 tablesp. chopped chives

The Pork Delivery

Like clockwork, right on the dot of one o'clock, every Thursday, he pushed open the kitchen door with one end of a side of pork and dumped it on the cold room floor. I was frantically trying to get out the lunch at that moment. I always panicked in case I hadn't enough, or good enough, food for the unknown gourmet at the other side of the kitchen wall.

So, when he said one day, 'Come here now, I want to tell ye something', I wasn't too quick to respond. But in spite of the rush, I listened for a minute, not wishing to be impolite. 'How much a pound are ye paying for yer pork?' he asked. I couldn't think. 'Well, if ye'd only take the head as well, ye'd get more and ye'd pay less. There's yer docket now and take the head next week and see the difference.'

Next week in the midst of my rush, I had to stop to scrutinise the docket. Yes, certainly, a side of pork with a half-head was costing me 4p per pound less than one without, but I was buying more pounds. No time to work that one out.

He shuffled around, shaking the lapel of his coat in a deprecating way, 'It's lunchtime and I don't like to go into your dining-room in my old coat,' he said pointedly. Well of course, I didn't like *not* to take the hint either, so every Thursday, for a while, whatever about the saving in the pork bill, he was getting a pound's worth of lunch in my kitchen.

Then I had also the problem of what to do with half a pig's head. It had to be brined and made into brawn. There is not much meat in a head, and it is very gelatinous, so if you wish, you can cook a small boiling fowl, ox tongue or piece of beef with it to add bulk and improve the texture. Crúibíns (pigs' trotters) are also boiled in the pot for extra meat and gelatinous properties.

Potted Meats

The best potted meats are made with equal quantities of lean meat and clarified butter. You can cut the butter down to half this quantity with better results for picnicking, so the paste will not soften too much on a warm day. Meat paste will keep very well in a fridge, more than a week anyway. If you are sure to eat it within a day or two, you can incorporate fresh, chopped herbs, but otherwise it must be only dried spices. Packed into individual pots, it can make a good and trouble-free starter for dinner as well as being excellent for picnics and snack meals.

Serve with fresh white bread or toast.

Brawn

Serves 3. Put head with water, herbs and spices into a saucepan just big enough to take it. Bring to the boil and simmer very gently for 3-4 hours or until the skin is loose and the flesh will come away easily from the bone. Skin it, remove all edible flesh and cut it into dice. Put in a bowl. Reduce cooking liquid to 1.2 litre/2 pt/5 cups approx. and pour over the brawn to cover generously. Leave to cool and set.

½ pig's head, lightly brined
1-2 crúibíns (pig's trotters)
4 l/6-8 pt/16-20 cups water
2 sprigs of sage
2 bay-leaves
20 peppercorns
6 cloves
½ teasp. juniper berries

To Salt Half a Pig's Head

Rub the dry ingredients into both sides of the head and leave it to soak in them for 4-7 days. Turn the head every day and rub in any undissolved salt and spoon over the juices.

¼ lb salt
1 level teasp. saltpetre
½ teasp. allspice
¼ teasp. ground black pepper

Potted Meat Paste

Melt the butter and strain it through muslin or a filter. Chop up the meat. Sprinkle with a little of the spice and salt. Blend all ingredients except about 2 tablespoons of butter in an electric liquidiser or food processor. Taste carefully and adjust seasoning and spices. Pack into a jar. Spoon the remaining butter over the jar to make a seal. Refrigerate until needed.

225 g/½ lb cooked cold meat, without fat
125 g/4½ oz/9 tablesp. butter
pinch of ground cloves, allspice and/or nutmeg
salt
small piece of muslin or filter paper

Pork and Bacon

When we buy a side of pork, the best cuts are usually scored, sprinkled with salt and fresh herbs, or spiked with garlic, and roasted. The shoulder is casserole roasted with herbs and vegetables and served with a creamy mustard and cider sauce.

We also make our own black puddings, sausages, and a pâté from the liver.

Bacon cures vary from country to country. Originally a way of preserving the meat, nowadays it often does not keep well.

Sorry to hear your son has gone to get cured...

Bacon Chop

Serves approx. 4-5. Use freshly-cured green bacon. Remove bones and cover bacon with cold water. Bring to the boil. If the bacon is salty, throw out the water and start again. Boil for 30 minutes approx. or until partly cooked. Remove rind and trim away surplus fat. Slice into chops 2 cm/½-1 in thick. Dip in flour, brush with beaten egg and coat with crumbs. Fry until cooked through and golden on both sides. Serve with Irish Mist or Redcurrant Sauce.

900 g/2 lbs loin of bacon (without the streaky end)
1 tablesp. flour
1 egg
dried crumbs

Glazed Ham or Glazed Loin of Bacon

Allow approx. 140 g/5 oz per person. Boil ham or bacon until nearly cooked. Remove rind, cut fat in a diamond pattern and stud with cloves. Blend brown sugar to a paste with a little pineapple juice. Spread this over the ham. Bake in a moderately-hot oven, 190°C/375°F/Regulo 5, for 20 minutes or until the top has caramelised. Baste with juices occasionally.

To boil a ham, allow 25 minutes per .5 kg/lb. To boil a loin of bacon, allow 20 minutes per .5kg/lb.

This is delicious on a cold buffet when cooked the same day. Cold buffet food is best freshly cooked and not too cold.

good quality fresh green ham or bacon or smoked bacon
1 small tin pineapple
brown sugar
cloves

Sausages (skinless)

For .5 kg/1 lb sausages. Mince the pork. Chop herbs finely and mix through crumbs. Crush garlic with salt to a paste. Beat egg. Mix all ingredients together thoroughly. Adjust seasoning. Fill into a piping bag fitted with a 2.5 cm/1 in plain nozzle. Pipe onto a floured board and cut into required lengths.

250 g/½ lb lean pork
250 g/½ lb pork fat
1 clove garlic
1-2 teasp. thyme, marjoram, basil, rosemary, mixed
1 egg
125 g approx./4-5 oz/1¼ cups soft breadcrumbs
salt and pepper

Vegetables

KEVIN DUNNE

Taste and Timing

Heaven knows, we all have our failures. As a very young bride, even then on the theory that good simple meals were best, I decided that a slab of cheese, some chutney, and boiled potatoes would suffice for lunch. Somehow, I failed to manage to cook the potatoes in time. I hadn't bread, so when my husband came home he had to be happy with just cheese, chutney and me.

These moments are balanced out quite unexpectedly. There was the day the American visitor stopped after his first mouthful of lunch and said in amazement, 'Why these carrots taste just like ... er ... carrots!'

Of course, there is a good reason for everything. If I had put my potatoes on to cook rather more than 10 minutes before lunchtime, we would have had potatoes. If I had put my carrots in a saucepan full of water and left them there as long as the potatoes should have been on, they would not have tasted half so carroty.

Concentrating Flavour in Vegetables

There are two ways of getting carrots to taste like carrots, or sprouts like sprouts, or any vegetable like its very own self.

1. Put vegetables in a saucepan and half-cover with boiling salted water. Put the lid on, turn them, watch them and finally when they are nearly done, remove the lid and evaporate the remaining water as fast as you can.

Brussels sprouts should take 5-10 minutes. Carrots should not be left whole unless they are small. Cut beetroot into cubes. They are most spectacular as first the red runs out into the water, but as the water boils away the colour is absorbed back into the beetroot. So are the flavour, the minerals and the vitamins — but you don't see them.

2. By far the simplest way to deal with vegetables is to put them into a heavy cast-iron casserole with a heavy, tight-fitting lid, salt and pepper. Cover with a butter-wrapper and sweat them in butter until soft on a very low heat or in a moderate oven. You can of course add chopped herbs. For instance, try mint with your cucumber and thicken the juices with a little roux. Marrows, courgettes, celery, leeks and cucumbers are very good done in this way. (Slice the leeks into 1 cm/½ in. rings first.)

Cooking Mushrooms

If you get field mushrooms or the exotic oyster mushrooms, simply season them and fry gently in butter. With cultivated mushrooms, freshness is vitally important. Button mushrooms are quite hard to cook right through and a short cooking period is essential. Therefore it is best to quarter or slice them. The medium-sized open flats have the best flavour and are cheaper to buy as they shed their spores and discolour in transport. These can be cooked like field mushrooms or are good stuffed.

When frying mushrooms, do not over-fill the pan or they will weep and stew in their own liquid rather than fry. Do not use too much fat and do not put on too fast a heat. If they are cooking dry, cover with a lid for 1-2 minutes and then remove it to evaporate any surplus liquid.

Cauliflowers

Take a head with leaves left on. Trim off the damaged ones. Wash and shred the remaining leaves, removing middle rib. Take a saucepan that exactly fits the cauliflower head and boil 1 in water in it. Put in shredded leaves, a little salt and sit cauliflower on top, stem down. Cover closely. Control heat so that it does not boil dry. Remove from pot when stalks are barely tender.

To Serve: Break heads into portions, dip in melted butter and serve with or without chopped leaves.

or

Bind leaves and coat heads in a sauce made of the cooking water mixed with a light cream, thickened with roux.

Cauliflower Cheese

Cook as above. To every 250 ml/½ pt/1 cup of cooking water add 250 ml/½ pt/1 cup of rich milk. Thicken with roux and add 70g/2½ oz/1 cup grated cheese.

To serve: Sit cauliflower on a bed of green leaves bound with sauce. Coat head with more sauce. Sprinkle with grated cheese and buttered crumbs. Reheat and brown top.

Tomato Dishes Cooked in Advance

All these tomato dishes can be cooked in advance.

Tomatoes can be stuffed with any buttered vegetable.

I was amazed when I first read about tomato fondue, as I had been making it for years. With all the essential ingredients to hand, it was an obvious way of cooking them. I thought I had a unique dish!

Tomato, Cheese and Onion

Serves 4-6. Add 2 cups grated cheese to Tomato Fondue recipe and stir in. This was a Friday dish in our household when fish was scarce.

Tomato Fondue
140 g/5 oz/2 cups grated cheese

Jerusalem Artichokes

705 g/1 lb 9 oz/5 cups chopped
  artichokes
110 g/4 oz/1 cup chopped onion
15 g/½ oz/1 tablesp. butter, good
  dripping or bacon fat
stock
2 teasp. finely-chopped parsley
French mustard

Serves approx. 6-8. Sweat onion in a little butter, bacon fat or a good dripping. Add artichokes. Barely cover with a good stock — not too salty. Boil until vegetables are soft and stock reduced to a glaze. Adjust seasoning. Stir in a little French mustard and chopped parsley.

Tomato Fondue

900 g/2 lbs very ripe tomatoes
110 g/4 oz/1 cup sliced onions
1 large clove garlic, crushed
1 dessertsp. oil
1 tablesp. any of the following:
  chopped thyme, parsley, mint,
  basil, lemon balm, marjoram
pepper, salt, sugar

Serves approx. 6. Sweat onions and garlic in oil. Peel and slice tomatoes and add to onions. Season with salt, pepper and sugar, and add a generous sprinkling of chopped herbs. Cook until soft. Adjust seasoning.

Tomatoes Stuffed with Herbs and Onions

Allow per person:
1 tomato
1-2 spring onions
½ teasp. butter
½ teasp. mixed fresh herbs
  (thyme, basil, lovage, lemon
  balm, parsley)
2 teasp. cream
2 teasp. grated Gruyère cheese
roux

Party quantities for 20:
20 tomatoes
340 g/12 oz/1½ cups spring
  onions, chopped in 7 mm/¼ in
  pieces
30 g/1 oz/2 tablesp. butter
1 tablesp. chopped herbs
250 ml/8 fl oz/1 cup sieved
  tomato liquid
salt, pepper, sugar
120 ml/4 fl oz/½ cup cream
2 tablesp. grated Gruyère cheese

Cut tops off tomatoes. Scoop out pips, liquidise and rub the liquid through a sieve. Season the tomato cases with salt, pepper and sugar. Slice up spring onions, including the green tops, and sweat them in butter. After 10 minutes pour in sieved tomato liquid. Reduce for 5-10 minutes. Add cream, herbs and cheese and thicken with roux. Fill this mixture into tomato cases. Replace top and bake in moderately-hot oven, 190°C/375°F/Regulo 5 for approx. 15 minutes, until soft but not broken.

Stuffed Mushrooms

Serves approx. 8. Mix all ingredients together. Fill into flat mushrooms. Spread with sauce and top with cheese and crumbs mixed. Cook 15 minutes at 200°C/400°F/Regulo 6. The tops should be lightly browned.

approx. 8 flat mushrooms
110 g/4 oz/1¼ cups chopped mushrooms
2 tablesp. breadcrumbs
1 tablesp. melted butter
1 egg yolk
1-2 teasp. cream
1-2 teasp. chopped chives
1-2 chopped parsley
1 clove garlic, crushed
salt and pepper

Coating:
55 g/2 oz/½ cup buttered crumbs
120 ml/4 fl oz/½ cup white sauce
30 g approx./1 oz approx./½ cup grated cheese

Mushrooms à la Crème

Serves 4. Fry onions in butter until soft. Remove. Fry mushrooms a few at a time, just covering the bottom of the pan. Take them off as soon as they go limp. Add more butter if necessary, but never too much. When cooked, add herbs and cream and a squeeze of lemon juice. Taste for seasoning. Thicken if necessary with roux.

450 g/1 lb/5 cups mushrooms, sliced
250 ml/8 fl oz/1 cup cream
1 tablesp. chives, chopped (optional)
170 g/6 oz/1½ cups onion, finely chopped
40 g approx./1-2 oz/2-4 tablesp. butter

parsley
lemon juice
salt and pepper

Buttered Cucumber

Serves approx. 4. Sweat diced cucumber in butter for 20 minutes approx. or until soft. Stir in snipped fennel and thicken with roux. Season.

30 g/1 oz/2 tablesp. butter
1 cucumber
½ teasp. snipped fennel
salt and pepper

Cucumber with Tomato and Mint

Serves approx. 5. Scald and peel the tomatoes. Cut them up finely and season with salt, pepper and sugar. Peel and chop the onion finely. Peel the cucumber and cut it into neat dice, the same size as lump sugar (1 cm/⅓ in approx.). Melt the butter in a heavy casserole. Add the chopped spring onion, including part of the green top. Cook until soft. Stir in tomatoes and cucumbers and cook gently for approx. 20 minutes or until cucumber is tender. Put a cover on the pot if it is getting too dry; you will need a little juice, but not too much. Finally stir in the cream and chopped mint. Taste and adjust seasoning.

4 tomatoes
2 spring onions
1 cucumber
30 g/1 oz/2 tablesp. butter
120 ml/2 fl oz/¼ cup cream
2 teasp. finely-chopped mint

Eileen and the Potatoes

I found it really impossible to keep a house this size and look after six children single-handed. Fortunately, somebody always turned up to help. One year it was Eileen. She was cheerful, quick and intelligent; I became dependent on her. One week she asked for her half day on a Wednesday instead of a Thursday and I didn't see her again for some while. Neither did her mother. We didn't know where she was, but on Wednesdays the boat sailed for England and someone saw her on the quays. A month later, she turned up as unexpectedly as she had left and tearfully came to see me. 'Well if you went to London,' I said, 'why did you come back again?' 'I couldn't eat the potatoes,' she sobbed.

Potatoes are really important to Irish people. British Queen are the ones we like to eat in summer and Kerr's Pink followed by Golden Wonder in winter. They are very floury and inclined to break in the cooking water. They should never be peeled before cooking. If they still break, the water must be poured off before they are quite cooked and the potatoes finish cooking in their own steam. They are peeled at table and (ideally) eaten with a big lump of golden butter.

There are a great many Irish potato dishes and some confusion about their names. The two we usually serve are Colcannon which is made with cabbage, and Stelk or Champ made with chives or spring onions.

Colcannon

Scrub potatoes and boil in salted water. Quarter, core and finely shred cabbage. Put in a very little boiling water. Boil rapidly, turning occasionally until cooked, and the water has all evaporated. Peel potatoes and mash with milk. Stir in cabbage immediately and heat very well. Taste for seasoning. Serve in a warm dish, hollowing the centre a little. The butter is placed in the hollow to melt slowly into the vegetables.

6-8 potatoes
1 head of cabbage
350 ml/12 fl oz/1½ cups milk
* approx.*
salt and pepper
70 g approx./2-4 oz/4-8 tablesp.
* butter*

Champ or Stelk

If onions are used, cook until soft in the milk. Peel and mash freshly-boiled potatoes and mix with milk and onions or with hot milk and raw chives. Season to taste.

6-8 potatoes
110 g/4 oz/1 cup chopped spring
* onions*
or
45 g/1½ oz/½ cup chopped
* chives*
350 ml/12 fl oz/1½ cups milk
* approx.*
70 g approx./2-4 oz/4-8 tablesp.
* butter*
salt and pepper

Leek, Potato and Cheese Pie

Serves 6-8. Wash leeks and cut into rounds, 1 cm/½ in thick. Peel and cut up potatoes to match the leeks. Melt butter in casserole. Toss vegetables in it and season them. Cover with a butter-wrapper and a heavy lid, and bake slowly until soft. Make a cheese sauce, adding a little crushed garlic to it. Mix with the vegetables and top with more grated cheese. It can be left like this until required. Cook in a moderately-hot oven, 190°C/375°F/Regulo5, until heated through and brown on top.

8 leeks
2 potatoes
45 g/1½ oz/3 tablesp. butter
salt and pepper
470 ml/16 fl oz/2 cups cheese
* sauce*
½ clove crushed garlic
2 tablesp. grated cheese

Pommes Duchesse

A dressed-up version of mashed spuds. Boil the potatoes in their jackets. Peel, mash and weigh them. Enrich them by beating in to each pound, 1-3 egg yolks or 1 whole egg and 1 yolk, 40g approx./1-2 oz/2-4 tablesp. butter, 2-3 tablespoons cream, enough hot milk to soften the mixture sufficiently for piping, and salt and pepper to taste.

Cooking Beetroot

I meet quite a few people who buy only bottled beetroot, simply because they can never get the red to stay inside the (genuinely) ruddy things.

I don't think peeling, chopping and cooking them as on page 106 is at all the best way if they are for a cold beetroot salad. If this is your problem, go about it in this way.

Leave 5 cm/2 in of leaf stalks on top and the whole root on the beet. Hold it under a running tap and wash off mud with the palms of your hands, so that you do not prick the skin. Cover in boiling water into which a little salt and sugar are added. Cover the pot and simmer on top, or in an oven, for 2-4 hours. They are done if they dent when pressed with a finger. If, after all this, the water is red and the beets pale pink inside, just put them back on. Remove the lid and boil them dry. The colour will return to them as the water evaporates. Occasionally in spring when the beets are old, they will not respond to this treatment, so boil more than you need.

Dressing Beetroot

225 g/8 oz/1 cup sugar
500 ml/16 fl oz/2 cups water
250 ml/8 fl oz/1 cup vinegar

For 500 g/1 lb beetroot, approx. 5 servings. Dissolve sugar in water, bringing it to the boil. Add vinegar, pour over peeled, sliced beets and leave to cool.

Cole Slaw

½ white cabbage with good heart
1 apple, grated
1 tablesp. raisins
small sprig of mint
few chopped chives
2 tablesp. honey
½ tablesp. white vinegar

Cut cabbage in quarters. Wash it well and discard the coarser outside leaves. Cut away stalk and with a very sharp knife shred the heart very finely. Put in a bowl with the other ingredients, and toss in a dressing made of honey and vinegar blended together.

Cauliflower Salad

1 head cauliflower
120 ml/4 fl oz/½ cup French dressing

Ideally this should be made with slightly-shot heads at the end of the season. Cook them as described. Divide the florets. Dip each into French dressing and arrange like a wheel on a round plate. Build up layer upon layer to reform the cauliflower head. This looks good on a cold buffet and is extremely easy.

Mushroom Salad

Serves 4-6. Follow recipe for Mushrooms à la Crème, using oil instead of butter. The onions should be slightly burned in oil. Do not thicken juices. Add crushed garlic, lemon and seasoning to taste.

170 g/6 oz mushrooms
1 small onion
2 tablesp. olive oil
lemon juice
1 small clove garlic

Carrot and Apple Salad

Mix ingredients together and toss in honey and vinegar dressing as for Cole Slaw. Best if prepared just before it is required. Measure honey and water generously if using metric measures.

140 g/5 oz/2 cups carrot, grated
225 g/8 oz/2 cups apple, grated
or
110 g/4 oz/1 cup celery, finely chopped
85 g/3 oz/1 cup cucumber, grated (optional)
2 tablesp. honey
½ tablesp. white vinegar

Onions Monégasque

Serves approx. 6. This can be made with larger onions if they are cut length-wise so that each segment has a piece of root left on, which will hold the leaves together. Put all ingredients in a saucepan together and stew gently until the onions are soft.

450 g/1 lb button onions
350 ml/12 fl oz/1½ cups water
115 ml/4 fl oz/½ cup white vinegar
3 teasp. olive oil
2 tablesp. sugar
250 ml/8 fl oz/1 cup tomato purée
½ bay-leaf
½ teasp. thyme
sprig of parsley
85 g/3 oz/½ cup seedless raisins
salt and pepper

Potato Salad

Potatoes are best tossed in French dressing while they are still hot. They can then be kept for a day or two without losing flavour.

Hot Potato Salad

Hot potato salad goes well with sausages, boiled bacon, pork or hot spiced beef. Red cabbage and a glass of beer would complete a good meal.

Sausages, bacon and pork also go well with a hot purée of potato and apple mixed in equal proportions.

Piped Potato Salad

The cold mashed potato salad is very useful for piping around platters of cold meats, fish and vegetable salads. Use a 1 in star nozzle for large dishes and a ½ in with a rather open tip for bordering scallop shells. The shells can be filled with a variety of different things such as shellfish, smoked ham or salmon, eggs, tomatoes, spring onions, watercress, lettuce etc. They can be prepared about an hour in advance without spoiling. Cover with wet grease-proof paper or damp muslin and keep cool. They make a delicious and very pretty starter for dinner.

Potato and Thyme Salad: Mr Sean O'Craidain's Recipe

He tells me that his mother made her potato salad this way, which proves that some enlightened pre-war households did, in fact, understand that oil was for more and better things than sunburn!

Potato Salad

Serves approx. 6. The potatoes should be boiled in their jackets and peeled, diced and measured while still hot. Mix immediately with French dressing, onion and parsley. Add salt and freshly-ground pepper and finally the mayonnaise. Keeps well for 2 days.

1 generous l/scant quart/4½ cups freshly-cooked diced potatoes (allow generous kg/2¼ lbs raw potatoes approx.)
1 tablesp. chopped parsley
1 tablesp. chopped chives, scallions or onion
120 ml/4 fl oz/½ cup French dressing
120 ml/4 fl oz/½ cup mayonnaise
salt and pepper

Hot Potato Salad

Make as above, adding diced eggs, gherkins and capers, but omit the mayonnaise.

ingredients as above
2 hard-boiled eggs
2 tablesp. gherkins
1 tablesp. chopped capers

Potato Salad Border

Mix all ingredients together, making sure there are no lumps or large pieces of herbs to stick in the pipe. Fill into a forcing bag filled with a 2.5 cm/1 in star nozzle. Use to decorate platters of cold meats and salads.

450 g/1 lb/2 cups mashed potato
2 tablesp. French dressing
2 tablesp. mayonnaise
1 tablesp. finely-chopped parsley
1 tablesp. finely-chopped chives

Potato and Thyme Salad

Serves approx. 6. Coat diced potatoes in a good oil. Season to taste and sprinkle liberally with freshly-picked thyme leaves.

1 kg/2 lbs approx./4½ cups cooked potatoes
120 ml/4 fl oz/½ cup oil
2-3 teasp. thyme leaves
salt and pepper

Green Salads

It seems to me that green salads arrived on Irish tables after the last war. Talk of raw food and Vitamin C, a belated realisation that oil was for eating or perhaps a faltering step towards sophistication — all those brought us fresh green dishes.

You will need lettuce as the basis of your salad and as many other green, white or near-green raw vegetables as you can get. Putting in tomato and carrot is cheating and not allowed, but you can put in finely-chopped parsley, mint or other herbs, spring onions, or grated onions, cucumber, mustard and cress, watercress, the white tips of cauliflowers, chopped celery, chopped endives, and tips of purple sprouting broccoli.

Toss with French dressing just before serving.

Tomato Salad

Firm but ripe tomatoes make the best salad. Sometimes one finds rather small, sweet fruit with green streaks on the skin near the calix: they usually come from cold houses with a rather low production. Do not peel them; the skin will be crisp and pleasant to eat and the fruit deliciously sweet.

Soft ripe tomatoes also make a good salad, but they must be dipped for an instant in boiling water and then peeled. Do not leave them sitting in the water or the flesh will become disgustingly mushy.

Red Cabbage

My neighbour, Else Schiller, taught me how to cook red cabbage. She explained to me that in Germany, where she came from, she first went to the market stall to buy a head of cabbage. Next she carried the cabbage to the place where they sold apples. She got them to weigh the cabbage and give her an equal weight of apples. At home, she prepared the cabbage and put it in the pot with the water and flavourings. While the mixture was heating up, she peeled the apples, sat them on top, and covered the pot. She said it was important not to stir the apples in until the last moment, when the cabbage underneath had cooked.

Traditional Salad

Arrange lettuce leaves like a rose in a deep bowl — biggest leaves on the outside, small leaves in the centre. Scatter some or all of the following between the leaves:

Quartered hard-boiled eggs, quartered tomatoes, slices of cooked beetroot, slices of cucumber, cress, watercress, mustard leaves.

Serve with Lydia's Dressing.

Tomato Salad

Allow 1 or 2 tomatoes per person. Sprinkle with salt, sugar and several grinds of black pepper. Toss immediately in just enough French dressing to coat the fruit and sprinkle with some or all of the ingredients listed. Tomatoes must be dressed immediately they are cut to seal in their aroma.

For 6 tomatoes:
1 teasp. chopped basil, mint,
*   thyme or tarragon*
½ mild onion
*   or*
6 spring onions
*   or*
½ clove garlic
½ green pepper
¼ teasp. salt
black pepper
½ teasp. sugar

Turnips and Bacon

Boil turnips, season them using plenty of pepper and mash them. Fry bacon, remove from pan. Fry turnips in bacon fat, turning frequently as they brown. The flavour will improve enormously during this operation. Serve together. This is very much a peasant dish. It is served with the inevitable boiled potatoes or as a vegetable with meat or poultry.

Allow per person:
⅓-½ swede turnip
2 thick bacon rashers

Red Cabbage

Serves approx. 4. Remove the damaged outer leaves of the cabbage; quarter, clean and shred it. Put it in a saucepan with vinegar, sugar, salt and water. Bring to the boil.

Meanwhile, peel and core the apples. When they are ready, lay them on top of the cabbage and reduce the heat under the saucepan so that it is barely simmering. Cover the pan closely and continue cooking until tender and all the liquid is absorbed, 30 minutes approx.

450 g/1 lb red cabbage
450 g/1 lb apples
1 tablesp. vinegar
1 tablesp. sugar
1 level teasp. salt
120 ml/4 fl oz/½ cup water

A Chinese Puzzle

Since Chinese leaves are often cooked, but can also be eaten raw, it occurred to me that lettuce leaves which are usually eaten raw might also be quite good cooked. Right! Try them! The same can be said for watercress.

Knowing One's Onions

Cooking whole growing onions, complete with part of their green leaves, give a new dimension to every recipe that says 'take an onion'. My favourites are overgrown scallions, measuring about 1 in (2.5 cm) across the bulb. I found them grilled with about 2 in of green left on and served with tacos in Mexico. At home we sweat them in a tiny piece of butter and sprinkle them with thyme leaves.

Melted Lettuce

Serves 2. Melt butter in a frying pan. Put in the lettuce and keep turning it over with a wooden spoon until all the leaves have gone soft and limp. Season with salt and pepper and add mint. Serve immediately.

15 g/½ oz/1 tablesp. butter
285 g/10 oz/5 cups coarse outer lettuce leaves, cut in strips
2 teasp. finely-chopped mint
salt and pepper

Watercress Purée

Serves 4. Wash and chop the cress and put with water in a heavy saucepan with a tight-fitting lid. Cook on a moderate heat until soft, turning a couple of times during cooking. Allow 10 minutes approx. to cook.

    Stir in the butter. Sprinkle in flour. Stir over the heat until the mixture begins to thicken. Blend in the milk and bring to the boil, still stirring. Cook for 1-2 minutes and then serve.

225 g/8 oz/5 cups chopped watercress
1 tablesp. water
15 g/½ oz/1 tablesp. butter
1 level tablesp. flour
300 ml/½ pt/1¼ cups light cream

Buttered Onions

Peel and trim onions leaving root base intact. Melt butter in a heavy pot and toss the onions in it. Add thyme. Cover with a butter wrapper and a tight fitting lid. Cook on a low heat until soft. Then remove them to a serving dish. Boil down pot juices to a glaze and pour over onions.

250 g/½ lb/2½ cups button onions
40 g/½ oz/1 tablesp. butter
1 teasp. thyme leaves
salt and pepper

TIM ALLEN

Sweets
and
Ices

Stolen Fruits

If you want to make people enjoy rhubarb, use a good variety and make it sweet enough. The rhubarb we use came from my grandfather's stock which he planted on his farm outside Cork about 100 years ago. It is a delicious red variety with no name we can trace. There are several good kinds available today, however.

When I was about ten, I spent a month with a favourite cousin. We used to 'steal' rhubarb from his mother's garden and cook it for ourselves in her kitchen. This episode gave me a lasting love for rhubarb.

Fruit Compotes, Stock Syrup and Lemonade

The fruit is poached in a stock syrup. The one we use is made by boiling 570 g/1¼ lb/2½ cups sugar in .5 l/1 pt//2½ cups of water for 2 minutes. This will keep for about a week in a fridge.

I have kept a bottle of this handy in my kitchen for many years. Originally, I used it to mix with freshly-squeezed orange and lemon juice to make a drink for a packed lunch for school children (quickly made, vitamins intact!). We now serve the same drink from our bar and for children's teas. It is a pity one comes across so few good alternative drinks to alcohol.

Compote of Rhubarb, Redcurrants, Plums, Damsons and Blackcurrants

Cover fruit with stock syrup (see opposite). Poach very gently until fruit is soft. Cool and serve with cream.

Compote of Apples

Serves approx. 3. Boil sugar and geranium leaf in the water for 1-2 minutes to make a syrup. Peel the apples thinly, keeping a good round shape. Quarter them, remove the core and trim the ends. Cut into segments 5 mm/¼ in thick. Poach them in the syrup until translucent but not broken.

110 g/4 oz/½ cup sugar
250 ml/8 fl oz/1 cup water
2 large apples
1 sweet geranium leaf (optional)

Compote of Blackberries and Apples

Prepare the apples as above. 3-5 minutes before they have finished cooking, add the blackberries; simmer together, so that they are both cooked at once.

110 g/4 oz/½ cup sugar
250 ml/8 fl oz/1 cup water
110 g/4 oz/2 large apples
1 cup blackberries

Compote of Pears (White Pears)

Halve, peel thinly and core carefully, keeping a good shape. Put them in a pan which will just fit them nicely. Add the sugar, a few thin strips of lemon rind and the juice of the lemon. Cover with a well-fitting lid and cook gently until soft. Cool and serve. Dessert apples may be cooked like pears.

6 pears
1 lemon
110 g/4 oz/½ cup sugar

Chocolate Pears

Cook pears as previous recipe. Melt chocolate over hot water. Thin to coating consistency with pear liquid and coat pears carefully. Decorate with whipped cream and crystallised violets.

6 pears
55 g/2 oz/2 squares plain chocolate
30 g/1 oz/1 square unsweetened chocolate

Pears for Pudding

A pretty party sweet can be made from red and white pears arranged alternately in a round dish to form a wheel. The fruit should be decorated with strategically placed rosettes of whipped cream.

Fruit Fools

Each fruit requires a different recipe because of varying levels of acidity, natural sugar and water content. Certain fruits must be sieved or put through a mouli to get out skins and pips. Remember to rub through every possible bit of pulp when doing so, particularly with raspberries which would otherwise be too runny. Sometimes it is easier to get big quantities through a sieve if they are liquidised first. A liquidiser is the only satisfactory utensil for making raw blackberries into a purée. Blackcurrants and redcurrants can be frozen with their strings left on. They are easy to string while still frozen and there is always more time for these jobs later on.

Note: double cream whips to twice its volume.

You're a wonderful fool!

And you're a darling idiot yourself..

GOOSEBERRY

Blackberry

Pears in Port Wine (Red Pears)

Serves approx. 6. Prepare as for Compote of Pears. Pare one or two thin slices of peel from the lemon. Add with remaining ingredients. Cover saucepan and simmer until soft. Remove pears. Boil down the liquid until thick and syrupy. Spoon over pears. Chill and serve.

6 pears
110 g/4 oz/½ cup sugar
250 ml/8 fl oz/1 cup port
rind of lemon
pinch of cinnamon
250 ml/8 fl oz/1 cup water

Blackberry Fool

Serves approx. 5-6. Make a dry purée by cooking apples in 1 or 2 tablespoons of water on a low heat. Liquidise or sieve and sweeten to taste while still hot. Purée raw blackberries (see opposite) and add them with whipped cream to apple.

310-475 g/11-17 oz/3-5 cups blackberries
255 g/9 oz/1 cup very dry apple purée
110 g/4 oz/½ cup sugar
250 ml/8 fl oz/1 cup whipped cream

Rhubarb and blackcurrants are strong and acid, so they must somehow be well diluted. Cooking in a stock syrup and then stiffening them again with a little gelatine is one way. Otherwise, one must use a great deal of cream and egg white. The amount of cream used in a fool is up to one's own taste. I personally do not like them to be too rich. A recipe for a good shortbread biscuit to be served with a fool is found in the next section.

Note: Chill all fools for at least 6 hours before serving.

Blackcurrant or Rhubarb Fool

Cover the blackcurrants or rhubarb with stock syrup (see p. 199). Cook until soft, liquidise and measure. For each pint of purée, soften 2 teaspoons gelatine in a little water and blend with the purée. Check the set. It should be thick rather than stiff. When cool add up to an equal quantity of whipped cream or egg white or both, according to taste.

Blackcurrant or Redcurrant Fool

Follow the recipe for Raspberry Fool adding more syrup, cream and egg white until diluted to taste. This gives you a fool of raw fruit. Alternatively the currants can be cooked for a minute or two in the syrup before making into a purée.

Apple Snow

450 g/1 lb cooking apples
120 ml/4 fl oz/½ cup water
250 g/8 oz/1 cup approx. sugar
2 egg whites
digestive or shortbread biscuits

Serves approx. 6. Peel and core apples. Cut into thick chunks. Cook with sugar and water on a low heat in a covered pot. When soft, rub through a sieve or liquidise. Check for sweetness; beat in more sugar while purée is still hot, if it is needed. Stiffly beat the egg whites and fold them in carefully. Serve well chilled, with soft brown sugar and single cream. Children should be offered digestive biscuits to crumble over the top — this is one of life's pleasures!

Apple Purée

Make as above. Omit egg white.

Gooseberry Fool

Serves approx. 6. As the summer goes on and the gooseberries mature, less sugar is needed for this fool. Cook gooseberries in very little water. Watch that they do not burn. Sieve or mouli. Beat sugar into the hot purée (try approx. 225 g/8 oz/1 cup sugar to 470 ml/16 fl oz/2 cups gooseberries). When cold, mix with an equal quantity of stiffly-whipped cream and pour into a glass serving dish. Serve with biscuits handed separately.

480 g/1 lb 1 oz/4 cups gooseberries
450 g/1 lb/2 cups sugar approx.
60 ml/2 fl oz/¼ cup water
whipped cream
shortbread biscuits

Raspberry Fool

Serves approx. 4-5. Liquidise and then sieve raw fruit. Dissolve sugar in water. Boil for 1 minute and leave to cool. It should set to a jelly. Boil again, if it does not. Mix to taste with fruit and add whipped cream and stiffly-beaten egg white.

450 g/1 lb/4 cups raspberries
340 g/12 oz/1½ cups sugar
120 ml/4 fl oz/½ cup water
470 ml/16 fl oz/2 cups whipped cream
1 egg white

Orange Mousse with Chocolate Wafers

Serves 6-8. Dissolve gelatine in 3 tablespoons warm water. Wash and grate very finely rind of 2 oranges (1½ oranges if very big). Put with 2 eggs, 2 egg yolks and 3 tablespoons castor sugar in a bowl. Whisk to a thick mousse (over a saucepan of boiling water if you do not have an electric mixer). Squeeze juice from 2 oranges and the lemon, mix with gelatine and add water to make up to 300 ml/½ pt/1¾ cups fluid. Stir this into egg mixture and cool, stirring frequently. When cold, just before it sets, stir in whipped cream and the remaining 2 egg whites, beaten stiff. Pour into a glass bowl or individual glasses.

    Decorate with orange segments and sweetened whipped cream into which finely-grated orange rind has been stirred (orange cream).

    Chocolate wafers: melt the chocolate in a bowl over water. Stir until quite smooth. Spread on a flat piece of white notepaper. Mark into wafer shapes with a knife. Cool. Peel the paper off the chocolate. Use to decorate mousse.

1 level tablesp. gelatine
2 oranges
1 lemon
4 eggs
3 tablesp. castor sugar
250 ml/8 fl oz/1 cup whipped cream

1 orange
250 ml/8 fl oz/1 cup whipped cream
30-55 g/1-2 oz/1-2 squares plain chocolate

Mrs Baker's Crème Brulée

I don't know where Mrs Baker is now. She stayed only one night, long ago. She left this lovely recipe behind with me. She said she had cooked it for the Countess of Rosse. I think she got it from Constance Spry. It makes the nicest Crème Brulée. The top is like smooth, shining mahogany. It seals in the soft cream underneath. At first sight, people are puzzled as to how to get into it.

Crème Brulée

Serves approx. 4. Make at least 12 hours in advance. Heat cream but do not boil. Pour it slowly onto the yolks, beating all the time. Add ½ tablespoon sugar. Return to the saucepan and cook on a medium heat, stirring until it is thick enough to coat the back of a spoon. It must not boil. Pour into a serving dish and chill until next day.

2 egg yolks
280 ml/½ pt/1¼ cups double cream
½ tablesp. and 225 g/8 oz/1 cup sugar
water
120 ml/4 fl oz/½ cup whipped cream

To make the top: Dissolve remaining sugar in 80 ml/3 fl oz/⅓ cup water. Boil down until caramelised and brown in colour. Remove from heat and immediately spoon caramel over the top of the pudding. Cool. Pipe a line of whipped cream around edge to seal the joint where the caramel meets the side of the dish. Serve within 12 hours, or the caramel will melt.

To serve: Crack the top by knocking sharply with the back of the serving spoon.

Note: 2 yolks only just set the cream. Be sure to use big eggs and measure your cream slightly short of the 280 ml/½ pt/1¼ cup. The cream takes some time to thicken and usually does so just under boiling point.

If the custard is not properly set, or if the skin which forms on top while cooking is broken, the caramel will sink to the bottom of the dish. If this problem arises, freeze the pudding for 1-2 hours before spooning on the hot caramel.

A Soufflé Omelette

This is a delicious last-minute pudding. It is difficult to serve in a restaurant as it cannot be made in less than 10 minutes and with any hitch this could become a disastrous half hour.

One night this happened. Paddy, my fourteen-year-old apprentice chef and I worked as fast as we could but reports of the party's impatience kept coming to us. Finally, we got the enormous omelette (it was made in a big pan) safely onto its sugared paper. Paddy held the serving dish under the shelf while I began the complicated double turn of the omelette. When it got to the stage of its somersault onto the dish he was holding, it all became too frightening: a big boiling golden wave was heading straight for his unprotected hands. He screamed and let the dish drop, the omelette after it on the floor.

My son-in-law was in charge of the dining-room. He surveyed the scene and went straight to his difficult customers: 'I'm sorry, sir,' he said to the host without flicking an eyelid, 'but your omelette is in the middle of the kitchen floor!' They rocked with laughter and waited quite cheerfully for another one without a murmur.

You can eat off the floor in this place — and you may have to...

Catman

130

Soufflé Omelette

Serves approx. 4. Beat yolks with 2 tablespoons of sugar and a few drops of vanilla essence. Beat whites stiff. Fold into yolks. (In fact, I find it easier to fold the yolks into the whites.) Heat butter in a very clean 23 cm/9 in omelette pan, pour in mixture and cook over low heat for 3 minutes. Do not stir. Finish cooking by putting pan in a hot oven for a further 3 minutes. Meanwhile boil fruit and 250 g/8 oz/1 cup sugar in a saucepan. Remove and add kirsch. Turn omelette onto brown paper well covered with castor sugar. Spread with warm fruit and cream. Quickly fold in two and turn again onto a warm dish. Sprinkle with more castor sugar.

4 egg yolks
6 egg whites
½ teasp. butter
450-680 g/1-1½ lb/2-3 cups castor sugar
170 g/6 oz/1½ cups soft fruit vanilla essence
½ tablesp. kirsch
120 ml/4 fl oz/½ cup whipped cream

Irish Mist or Sweet Geranium Soufflé

Serves approx. 6. This mixture can be filled into lemon skins or served as a soufflé. If filling lemons, cut the tops off, scoop out the insides and strain. Otherwise squeeze lemons in the ordinary way. Crush the geranium leaf in your hand and put it in the lemon juice. Beat egg yolks with sugar to a thick mousse using an electric mixer or by hand over a saucepan of boiling water. Add Irish Mist and beat again. Melt gelatine in 2 teaspoons of lemon juice and 1 tablespoon of water (page 10). Blend gelatine and remaining strained lemon juice with the mousse. Put the geranium leaf in, too, if you think enough flavour has not been extracted. Beat egg whites stiff and fold in. The sweet should be served semi-frozen.

10-14 lemons
4 eggs
1 large sweet geranium leaf (Pelargonium Graveolens)
1 tablesp. Irish Mist
4 tablesp. castor sugar
2 small lemons
2 teasp. gelatine

The Soufflé: These quantities make 1.2 l/2 pints/5 cups in volume, enough to fill a 900 ml/1½ pint/4 cup soufflé dish. Greaseproof paper should be tied round the soufflé dish to give it another 5 cm/2 in in height. You then over-fill the dish, freeze for 4 hours and remove the paper. Top with a rosette of whipped cream and a large geranium leaf.

The Lemons: Fill lemon skins with the mixture and freeze for 4 hours. You will have lemon pulp left over which can be strained and used for some other purpose such as in a drink.

Hot Lemon Soufflé

The recipe on the opposite page is not a true soufflé at all. I don't know where it came from. The pudding arrived in our household in the late 1930s, I think, amongst much excitement on the part of my mother and my aunts. It's funny to make, trying to cream so little butter into so much sugar, but it works. The top is light and spongy. The bottom is a sticky lemon sauce.

Lemon Soufflé

Serves approx. 4. Cream butter and sugar together. Add flour and beaten yolks. Blend in the juice and finely-grated rind of lemon, and then the milk. Stiffly beat the egg whites and fold them in. Pour into a baking dish and bake 40 minutes approx. at 180°C/350°F/Regulo 4 until set.

1 tablesp. softened butter
250 g/8 oz/1 cup sugar
2 tablesp. flour
2 eggs
1 lemon
250 ml/8 fl oz/1 cup milk

Chocolate Soufflé

Put chocolate, rum and 1 tablespoon water in a saucepan; melt over a very low heat. Put gelatine in a bowl with 2 tablespoons water and dissolve over a saucepan of boiling water (page 10). Beat 3 eggs and 2 yolks with sugar to a stiff mousse. Blend in gelatine and chocolate. Cool and add whipped cream. Whip stiffly the remaining two egg whites and fold in carefully.

Tie a band of greaseproof paper around a 500 ml/1 pt/2½ cup soufflé dish, to come 7.5 cm/3 in over the top. Fill mixture in; it should come at least 1 cm/½ in over the top of the bowl. Refrigerate for 6 hours. Remove paper band and decorate as desired before service.

85 g/3 oz/3 squares plain
  chocolate
30 g/1 oz/1 square unsweetened
  chocolate
3 tablesp. rum
1 tablesp. water
7.5 g/¼ oz./1 tablesp. gelatine
5 eggs
70 g/2½ oz/5 tablesp. castor
  sugar
350 ml/12 fl oz/1½ cups whipped
  cream

Caramel Mousse

Dissolve sugar in 120 ml/4 fl oz/½ cup of water and boil until it turns to a chestnut brown. Remove from heat. Immediately add 150 ml/¼ pt/⅝ cup hot water. Reheat to dissolve caramel. You should now have a thickish caramel sauce. Pour slowly onto egg yolks, beating all the time. Continue beating to a bulky mousse. Dissolve gelatine in 30 ml/1 fl oz/⅛ cup water. Blend this in with the mousse. Add cream. Pour into serving dish and chill.

225 g/½ lb/1 cup sugar
  water
4 egg yolks
2 teasp. gelatine
300 ml/½ pt/1¼ cup whipped
  cream

Ballyandreen

Ballyandreen is a tiny fishing village by a rocky inlet four miles south of Ballymaloe. For generations the inhabitants there have gathered and sold carrageen moss. It is picked from the farthest out rocks at low water during spring tides in June. This means that it is almost always covered by sea water. It is then laid out on the short grass on the clifftop to dry and bleach in the sun. It has the reputation of being a health-giving food. It is a source of agar jelly. It certainly contains iron and minerals. Traditionally, it was fed to calves and made into cough syrups and milk puddings. I have used it all my life. I have thickened milk for babies with it at weaning time. For more sophisticated meals I serve it topped with whipped cream and coffee sauce strongly laced with whiskey.

Chocolate Carrageen has nostalgic memories for me. I first encountered it at Sunday night supper in this house, long ago, when it was still clad in its Victorian decor and life was very different.

A product that is hard to measure, however, is hard to market. This is so with carrageen moss. The success of this dish is in using only just enough to get a set — so that you don't taste it in the pudding, as an unenthusiastic friend pointed out!

Carrageen sometimes comes mixed with grass and other seaweeds; these should be carefully removed before use.

Picking Carrageen

There are two very similar varieties of carrageen moss, *Gigartina stellata* and *Chondrus crispus.* Both are widely distributed.

They are brownish black or dark green and from 7.5-15cm/3-6 in long. They grow abundantly on the rocks at low tide line.

Pick in early summer at low water during spring tides. Bleach in the sun. Wash occasionally in plenty of cold water then lay out to dry again. When quite white and well dried, bring indoors and store in a jute bag. It will keep for one or two years.

Carrageen for a Dinner Party

Make a Carrageen Moss Pudding. Set in a shallow bowl.

Make a rather thick Irish Coffee Sauce. When cold it should coat the back of a spoon. Lay a 7 mm/¼ in. layer of this carefully over the top of the carrageen and top with a layer of whipped cream.

Carrageen Moss Pudding

Serves 4-6. Soak the carrageen in tepid water for 10 minutes. Put in a saucepan with milk and a vanilla pod if used. Bring to the boil and simmer very gently for 20 minutes. Pour through a strainer into a mixing bowl. The carrageen will now be swollen and exuding jelly. Rub all this jelly through the strainer and beat it into the milk with the sugar, egg yolk and vanilla essence, if used. Test for a set in a saucer as one would with gelatine. Whisk the egg white stiffly and fold it in gently. It will rise to make a fluffy top. Serve chilled with a fruit compote, Caramel or Irish Coffee Sauce.

7 g/¼ oz/½ cup cleaned, well-dried carrageen (1 semi-closed fistful)
925 ml/1½ pt/3¾ cups milk
2 tablesp. sugar
1 egg
½ teasp. vanilla essence or vanilla pod

Chocolate Carrageen

Serves 4-6. Proceed as for plain carrageen. Blend cocoa with a little of the milk and add to hot, strained carrageen before adding the egg. Chill well. Best eaten next day. Note that double the amount of carrageen is needed when cocoa is added.

15 g/½ oz/1 cup cleaned, well-dried carrageen (2 semi-closed fistfuls)
925 ml/1½ pt/3¾ cups milk
2 tablesp. sugar
½ teasp. vanilla essence or vanilla pod
3 tablesp. cocoa
Warning: cocoa heaps easily on a spoon; watch the measurement

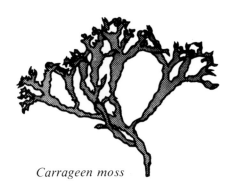

Carrageen moss

Sweet Sauces

The sauces opposite are good accompaniments for certain plain sweets. Any of them will improve a block of bought vanilla ice cream. Try a Caramel or the Irish Coffee Sauce with Carrageen Moss Pudding. Try Caramel Sauce with rice or custard puddings, or Irish Mist with plum puddings or bacon chop. Try Coffee Sauce with or without the whiskey for coffee ice cream.

The Chocolate Sauce separates if left standing for a while, so beat it up before use. It is good with vanilla ice cream and pears or poured over profiteroles. Use the best quality plain dark chocolate. This and unsweetened chocolate are obtainable from good delicatessens.

Chocolate Sauce

Melt the chocolate in a bowl over simmering water. Gradually stir in the syrup. Flavour with rum or vanilla essence.

55 g/2 oz/2 squares plain chocolate
30 g/1 oz/1 square unsweetened chocolate
175 ml/6 fl oz/³/₄ cup syrup approx.
rum or vanilla essence

Irish Mist Sauce

Cook sugar with water to a caramel. Pour in 2 tablespoons whiskey and 2 tablespoons Irish Mist. Simmer until caramel is dissolved. Add a little water if necessary.

225 g/8 oz/1 cup sugar
80 ml/3 fl oz/¹/₃ cup water
2 tablesp. whiskey
2 tablesp. Irish Mist

Irish Coffee Sauce

Make a caramel as above. Add coffee (made to drinking strength) instead of water. Cool and add whiskey.

225 g/8 oz/1 cup sugar
80 ml/3 fl oz/¹/₃ cup water
250 ml/8 fl oz/1 cup coffee
1 tablesp. Irish whiskey

Caramel Sauce

Dissolve sugar in 80 ml/3 fl oz/¹/₃ cup water over heat and continue cooking to a caramel. Remove from heat. Pour in 250 ml/8 fl oz/1 cup water and continue cooking until caramel is dissolved and smooth. Do not stir.

225 g/8 oz/1 cup sugar
330 ml/11 fl oz/1¹/₃ cups hot water

Ballymaloe Ice Creams

These ice creams are made on an egg mousse base with whipped cream and flavouring added. Ice creams made in this way have a smooth texture and do not need further beating during the freezing period.

They should not be served frozen hard. Remove from freezer at least 10 minutes before serving.

Butter by Mistake

Butter-making in the kitchen is not just a remote possibility.

While the cream is whipping in the mixer, there is just time to do something else. Take your eye off it for too long, and when you come back the cream looks funny, granular, wetter than expected and it does not taste right. If it is too far gone to pass for whipped cream, turn on the mixer again and in a few minutes you will have a lump of golden butter sloshing around in some buttermilk. Put it in a strainer and run a cold tap through it. Next turn it out on a wooden board placed on the draining board. With wet butter patties or two wooden spoons or spatulas, beat it, flatten it, box it. Keep throwing cold water over it to wash out the buttermilk. Finally salt it to taste. The best use for the buttermilk is to sour it for making soda bread.

Vanilla Ice Cream

Serves 6-8. Boil the sugar and water together to a thread. It will look thick and syrupy and when a metal spoon is dipped in, the last drops of syrup will form thin threads. Beat this a little at a time into the egg yolks. Add vanilla essence and beat to a thick creamy white mousse. Fold the cream in. Set to freeze.

2 tablesp. sugar
120 ml/4 fl oz/½ cup water
2 egg yolks
½ teasp. vanilla essence
620 ml/1 pt/2½ cups whipped cream

Chocolate Ice Cream

Serves 6-8. Make an egg mousse as for Vanilla Ice Cream. Melt chocolate in a cool oven or over boiling water. Stir this into the egg mousse. Fold in the cream and freeze. This is a very rich mixture.

Ingredients as above
55 g/2 oz/2 squares plain chocolate
30 g/1 oz/1 square unsweetened chocolate

Coffee Ice Cream

Serves 6-8. Prepare mousse as for Vanilla Ice Cream. Stir in instant coffee dissolved to a paste in water. Fold in the cream.

Ingredients as above but omit vanilla essence
3 teasp. instant coffee
½ teasp. boiling water

Caramel Ice Cream

Serves 6-8. Make a syrup as for Vanilla Ice Cream, but continue to boil until the sugar caramelises to a chesnut brown. Quickly pour on 120 ml/4 fl oz/½ cup of water. Do not stir, boil gently until it again becomes a smooth thick syrup. Pour this on egg yolks and finish as for vanilla ice cream.

Ingredients as above but omit vanilla essence

Praline Ice Cream

Serves 6-8. Make as for Vanilla Ice Cream. Freeze. When just beginning to set, fold in the praline. Put into moulds and freeze again.

2 tablesp. praline

To make praline: Put unpeeled almonds and sugar together in a small heavy saucepan. Heat until the sugar caramelises. Turn onto an oiled slab and crush to a coarse powder.

55 g/2 oz/⅔ cup almonds
55 g/2 oz/¼ cup sugar

Using Egg Whites

If you love to make emulsion sauces, that is Hollandaise, Béarnaise, Mayonnaise and so on, you have a problem. It is egg whites. Fortunately, they will keep some days in a jar in a fridge. Some can be used in batter, fruit fools, for beating into mashed potatoes, or glazing the tops of pies. After that, meringues it must be. Before you dream of trying them, do go out to search for silicone-finished paper (marketed as Bakewell Paper), or perhaps you might find a silicone baking sheet. It is quite possible to do without these, but the job is much more hazardous. The paper just pops up in a different place everytime. I have had it from London, Dublin, Cork and New York — quite a shopping feat I can tell you, when one is tied to a farm in the deep country of south east Cork. Fortunately, I have some friends around!

Note: If you cannot get silicone paper or a silicone baking sheet, grease and flour an ordinary baking sheet very thickly indeed. Oiled and floured tin foil can also be used.

Warning: The presence of any oil, grease or egg yolk will prevent egg whites from whipping to the correct consistency for meringues.

Coffee, nuts and orange rind all contain oil. The meringue will fail when these are added unless great care is taken to beat the whites to very dry stiff peaks before the final addition of sugar and flavouring. The meringues should then be got into the oven as quickly as possible before the oil starts to work on the mixture.

The white of one egg generally weighs 30 g/1 oz.

Almond Meringue Gâteau with Chocolate and Rum Cream

45 g/1½ oz/¼ cup almonds
2 egg whites
117 g/4½ oz/1 cup approx. icing sugar

Blanch and skin almonds. Grind or chop them up. They should not be ground to a fine powder but left slightly coarse and gritty. Mark two 19 cm/7½ in circles on silicone paper or a prepared baking sheet. Mix all the sugar with the egg whites at once and beat until the mixture forms stiff dry peaks. Fold in almonds. Spread and bake immediately in a moderate oven, 160°C/325°F/Regulo 3, for 30 minutes or until set crisp and just brown on top.

Filling:
30 g/1 oz/1 square plain chocolate
15 g/½ oz/½ square unsweetened chocolate
310 ml/½ pt/1¼ cups whipped cream
1 tablesp. rum
1 tablesp. single cream

Filling: Melt chocolate very gently in a very cool oven, or over hot water. Stir in rum. Blend with single cream and then fold mixture into a whipped cream.

To make up: Sandwich meringues together with filling. Chill for some hours before serving. Decorate with rosettes of chocolate cream stuck with halved baked almonds.

Basic Meringue

Serves 4-6. Beat whites until stiff but not yet dry. Fold in half sugar. Beat again until the mixture will stand in a firm dry peak. Fold remaining sugar in carefully. Pipe into required shapes or spread onto a silicone sheet of paper as required. Bake in a very low oven, 100°C/200°F/Regulo ½, 4 hours approx.

2 egg whites
110 g/4 oz/½ cup castor sugar

Meringue Gâteau

Serves 4-6. Divide basic mixture in two and spread inside two 19 cm/7½ in circles marked on a baking sheet. Bake as directed. Cool and sandwich with filling.

Filling:
85 g/3 oz/¾ cup fresh fruit
250 ml/8 fl oz/1 cup whipped cream
2 teasp. kirsch

Coffee Meringue

Serves 4-6. Proceed as for basic recipe until the dry peak stage is reached. Mix coffee with icing sugar. Sift and fold in very gently. Bake as directed.

Filling:
250 ml/8 fl oz/1 cup unsweetened whipped cream
1 tablesp. whiskey

2 egg whites
2 tablesp. castor sugar
2 tablesp. icing sugar
2 teasp. instant coffee

Walnut Meringue

Serves 4-6. Make as for basic meringue. Fold in nuts at the end. Bake as directed. Also good with hazel or brazil nuts.

Filling:
250 ml/8 fl oz/1 cup unsweetened whipped cream
1-2 ripe dessert pears

2 egg whites
110 g/4 oz/½ cup castor sugar
12 chopped walnut or brazil nut kernels

Orange Meringue

Serves 4-6. Make as for basic meringue. Fold in orange rind at the end. Bake as directed. Fill with orange mousse and decorate with orange segments and cream. We usually leave a hole in the centre of one meringue to be filled with segments.

Filling and decoration:
140 g/5 oz/1 cup orange mousse
skinned segments of 1 orange
120 ml/4 fl oz/½ cup unsweetened whipped orange cream

2 egg whites
110 g/4 oz/½ cup castor sugar
2 teasp. very finely-grated orange rind

Serving Ice Cream

It took me twelve years to find the solution to keeping ice cream cold on the sweet trolley in my restaurant. At first we used to unmould and decorate our ices onto a plate. This was alright on a busy night when they got eaten before melting. On quieter occasions the waitresses performed relay races from the dining-room to the deep freeze. I dreamed about 19th century ice boxes filled from ice houses, to my husband's increasing scorn, and then I thought I had a solution. A young Irish glass blower produced beautiful hand-blown glass cylinders which I filled with ice cream and fitted into beautiful tulip shaped glass bowls. These I filled with ice cubes. Six months later, however, due to either the stress of the ice or the stress of the waitresses, my bowls were gone and so was my money.

In desperation I produced an ice bowl. It turned out to be a stunning and practical presentation for a restaurant trolley or a party buffet. Piled up with ice cream and set on a folded serviette to absorb moisture, we surround it with vine leaves in summer, scarlet Virginia Creeper in autumn. We wipe it clean with a damp cloth; water puts holes in it. It can be used two or three times but gradually begins to look worn. If a serving spoon is left in it, it will melt a notch in the rim wherever it rests.

To Make an Ice Bowl

Take two bowls, one about double the capacity of the other. Do not use aluminium. Half fill the big bowl with cold water. Float the second bowl inside the first. Weight it down with water or ice cubes until the rims are level. Adjust so that the smaller bowl stays in a central position by sticking pieces of flour and water paste on to its rim to widen it enough to hold it in place. The water should come to within 1 cm/½ in of the top.

Alternative Method: Float second bowl so that its rim is 1 cm/½ above the rim of the big bowl. Place a square of fabric over the top and tie it on with string under the rim of lower bowl as one would tie on a jam pot cover. Adjust the small bowl to a central position. The cloth holds it in place.

Put the bowls in a deep freeze, if necessary re-adjusting the position of the small bowl as you put it in. After 24 hours turn out as follows.

Remove the cloth or wedges. Twist and shake the small bowl free of the ice bowl. Dip the big bowl for a second or two in warm water or leave at room temperature for ½ hour. Twist and shake the ice bowl free, and turn it out carefully. If disaster looms and the ice bowl splits, press it together firmly and put it back in the big bowl to refreeze for about 15 minutes.

The ice melts at the base where it touches the serving dish, so a thick-bottomed bowl is best. Serve on a folded serviette to absorb moisture.

Blackcurrant Ice Cream

Make an egg mousse as for Vanilla Ice Cream. Add to it a semi-sweet black-currant purée. The fruit can be raw and sweetened with a thick syrup or cooked in a syrup. Taste for sweetness after adding to the mousse, adding more syrup if necessary. Fold in cream. Set to freeze.

2 egg yolks
2 tablesp. sugar
120 ml/4 fl oz/½ cup water
280 ml/½ pt/1¼ cups blackcurrant purée
560 ml/1 pt/2½ cups whipped cream

Strawberry Ice Cream

Serves approx. 6. Dissolve sugar in 60 ml/2 fl oz/¼ cup water and boil for exactly 1 minute. Soften gelatine in 1 tablespoon water in a small bowl and dissolve over boiling water. When completely dissolved, gradually blend in the fruit purée. Add syrup and lemon juice to sharpen. Cool and add whipped cream. Set to freeze.

425 ml/14 fl oz/1¾ cups strawberry purée
110 g/4 oz/½ cup sugar
water
1 teasp. powdered gelatine
½ lemon
250 ml/8 fl oz/1 cup whipped cream

Raspberry Ice Cream

Make as for Strawberry Ice Cream. Lemon juice is not necessary.

Note: 450 g/1 lb raspberries or strawberries yield 500 ml/16 fl oz/2 cups approx. purée. Rub raw fruit through a sieve or spin in food processor. Pips may be strained out.

325 ml/14 fl oz/1¾ cups raspberry purée
285 g/10 oz/1¼ cups sugar
water
1 teasp. gelatine
600 ml/1 pt/2½ cups whipped cream

Unmoulding Ice Creams

One night in a great rush, my daughter Wendy, who managed my dining-room, rushed out for another ice cream. She picked a mould out of the deep freeze and held it upside down under the nearest hot tap. The ice cream obligingly popped out, but she hadn't time to catch it, and we watched helplessly as it was washed through a grating underneath. After that we always dipped our moulds in a bowl of hot water.

To unmould: Dip the mould for 5 seconds approx. in hot water. Take a thin-bladed knife and slip it down one side of the mould to the bottom and lever up a little to allow air underneath. Turn out onto a serving dish. The knife mark can be smoothed over.

The Bombe

The flavour of coffee and praline ice cream, inside a chocolate ice cream case, blend well together in this bombe. It is a good dinner party sweet. Serve it on a silver dish and decorate with praline, crystallised violets and whipped cream. Serve one or both sauces, separately. Smoothing the layers of ice cream onto the mould is a little tricky. If the ice gets soft, it will slide to the bottom of the mould. If this happens, turn the mould upside down on a plate and refreeze for 1 hour.

Whiskey Oranges

6 oranges
2 eggs
55 g/2 oz/$\frac{1}{4}$ cup sugar
150 ml/5 fl oz/$\frac{5}{8}$ cup milk
300 ml/$\frac{1}{2}$ pt/1$\frac{1}{4}$ cup whipped
 cream
3 level teasp. gelatine
2$\frac{1}{2}$ tablesp. Irish whiskey

For decoration:
150 ml/5 fl oz/$\frac{5}{8}$ cup whipped
 cream
24 fresh bay-leaves
2 tablesp. Irish whiskey

For 12 half oranges, boil sugar and milk together until thick. A drop falling from the side of a spoon should leave a slight thread. Separate yolks from the whites of eggs and add milk mixture gradually to yolks. Beat to a thick mousse. Squeeze juice from oranges and scrape the skins clean to leave nicely-shaped orange halves. Dissolve gelatine in a little of the orange juice in a cup or bowl over boiling water. Blend carefully with 150 ml/5 fl oz/$\frac{5}{8}$ cup of remaining juice. Cool. Add it with the whipped cream and liqueur to yolks. Whip egg whites stiffly and fold them in also. Fill into orange halves, heaping up as much as you can get in. Freeze for 2 hours.

To decorate: Pipe a line of whiskey-flavoured, sweetened whipped cream across the centre of each orange and stick 2 bay-leaves in either side.

The Bombe

Serves 6-8. Make the day before required. Make an egg mousse with sugar and water boiled to a thread, and egg yolks, as described for Vanilla Ice Cream. Divide mousse equally into three bowls. Melt chocolate, being careful not to over-heat. Stir melted chocolate into the first bowl, 1 tablespoon praline into the second, and instant coffee dissolved to a paste in boiling water, into the third bowl. Finally whip 300 ml/½ pt/1¼ cups cream for each bowl, and mix in thoroughly. Set the three bowls to freeze. When just frozen, take out the chocolate ice cream and work until pliable enough to coat the mould in an even layer. Return to the freezer for 2 hours. Repeat the process with the praline ice. After 2 hours, freeze again; fill the centre with the coffee ice. Leave overnight to set. Just before serving, whip remaining cream. Unmould the bombe and decorate it with remaining praline, cream and crystalised violets.

1.2 l/2 1/2 pt/5 cup mould
3 tablesp. sugar
60 ml/2 fl oz/¼ cup water
3 egg yolks
30 g/1 oz/1 square plain
  chocolate
15 g/½ oz/½ square unsweetened
  chocolate
1½ tablesp. praline
2 teasp. instant coffee
½ teasp. boiling water
1 l/1¾ pt/4⅓ cups cream
Irish Coffee Sauce or Chocolate
  Sauce with Rum
crystallised violets for decoration

Iced Chocolate Oranges

Serves approx. 6. Cut the tops off the oranges. Scoop out the pulp. Liquidise and sieve it. Sweeten with syrup to taste. You will need 370 ml/½ pt/1¼ cups for the sweet. Anything over can be used for drinks. Prepare an egg mousse as for Vanilla Ice Cream. Divide it into two bowls. Melt chocolate and add it to one bowl. Stir in half the whipped cream and half-fill the oranges. Freeze. Dissolve gelatine in 1 tablespoon of orange juice over hot water. Blend with the measured orange and add to remaining egg mousse. Fold in cream. Fill up the oranges and return to freezer. To serve, cut in quarters lengthwise and arrange on a serving dish decorated with orange segments, bay-leaves and orange-flavoured cream.

3-4 oranges
stock syrup
2 egg yolks
2 tablesp. sugar
600 ml/1 pt/2½ cups whipped
  cream
1 level teasp. powdered gelatine
30 g/1 oz/1 square plain
  chocolate
15 g/½ oz/½ square unsweetened
  chocolate

Iced Chocolate Cases with Rum Cream

For 12 cases. Spread a thin layer of melted chocolate inside a paper case of double thickness (i.e. one paper inside another). Let it cool and set. Fill to the top with semi-frozen chocolate ice cream. Freeze until well set. Peel off the papers. Top with a large rosette of whipped cream, lightly sweetened and flavoured with rum.

Approx. 225 g/½ lb chocolate coats 12 cases, and 470 ml/16 fl oz/2 cups of ice cream fills them.

225 g/½ lb chocolate approx.
24 small cake cases
470 ml/16 fl oz/2 cups chocolate
  ice cream
250 ml/8 fl oz/1 cup whipped
  cream
1 teasp. castor sugar
1 tablesp. rum

The End of an Era

Kathleen washes up for us. When Mrs Flower died, she was moved. 'That's the last of the old royalities,' she shouted to the young people in the kitchen, who didn't understand. The era was already gone.

Gone are the groups of gentry once found in the hotels, at the shows and races. Smart, jolly and self-assured, they were terrifyingly intimidating if you were not one of them. Gone are so many of the houses they came from, their furniture, their books and their beautiful walled gardens.

It was my lot to live on the fringes of this society. I sometimes received an invitation to one of the big houses. I particularly remember a June dinner-party at one such house. The final course was a melting strawberry sorbet. At another, I remember a wonderful loin of perfect local lamb. It had been boned and stuffed with buttery crumbs and fresh herbs from the garden, then rolled up and tied for roasting. Tiny scones with fresh homemade jam and thick cream instead of butter and deep soft sponge cakes were served for afternoon tea. It was on rare visits to these houses that I found a new dimension in Irish cooking.

Fruit Sorbets

All the following recipes are made without a machine. If using frozen fruit, put the fruit straight into the hot syrup. It will thaw and the syrup cool at the same time.

Marino House Strawberry Water-Ice

Hull and mash the strawberries with a fork or spin them in a liquidiser until they are in small pieces, stopping just before the purée stage. Boil the sugar and water for 2 minutes approx. Cool and add to the fruit with the juice of the lemon, tasting as you go to make sure the purée mixture is not too sweet. Stir well and freeze. When almost set, whip the egg whites very stiffly, add icing sugar and beat again. Take the strawberry mixture out of the freezer and beat it well in a chilled bowl to break up the ice crystals, but stop before it melts. Fold in the egg white and refreeze.

450 g/1 lb strawberries
225 g/8 oz/1 cup sugar
250 ml/8 fl oz/1 cup water
juice of ½-1 lemon
2 egg whites
1 tablesp. icing sugar

Blackberry Sorbet

Put geranium leaves and sugar into cold water. Bring them to the boil and make as directed for Strawberry Water-Ice.

450 g/1 lb blackberries
225 g/8 oz/1 cup sugar
250 ml/8 fl oz/1 cup water
5-6 sweet geranium leaves
2 egg whites
½ lemon (optional)

Gooseberry Sorbet

Serves 6. Put sugar, water and elderflowers into a saucepan. Bring to the boil slowly. Remove flowers, add gooseberries, and stew gently until soft. Strain off liquid, chill and freeze. (Remaining gooseberry pulp can be used for a fool.) When juice is frozen to a mush, beat it. Fold in stiffly beaten egg white. Refreeze until set.

450 g/1 lb/4 cups gooseberries
600 ml/1 pt/2½ cups water
225 g/8 oz/1 cup sugar
2 elderflower heads
1 egg white

The Pancake Blaze

Crêpe Suzette, the queen of the pancake family, is a party piece. It cannot be served to too many people at once, so it goes onto our menu around Shrove Tuesday time, when oranges are at their best and restaurant numbers are down. I usually have to dress up and cook the crêpes myself for the customers at table.

One evening I spruced myself up, put on a suitable little black dress, washed and set my hair so that it was all soft and fluffy and arrived in the dining-room ready for the performance. I proceeded to a table of about six people, all wanting crêpes. I followed the usual procedure of heating the pancakes on both sides in hot orange butter, folding them into fan shapes and arranging them around the edge of the pan, finally pouring in orange curaçao and brandy to flame them. Well, six people take quite a lot of pancakes, so I put in a good dash of the two liquors. They ignited with quite a bang — gave me a little shock, in fact, but naturally I proceeded with the cooking operation. After a minute, a waitress near me started to scream and a look of unusual consternation came over my customers. Then suddenly, a man jumped up from the table and enveloped my head in his serviette.

I didn't know that I was calmly cooking with a halo of flames engulfing my lovely fluffy hair.

'Sit down,' they said, 'You must be suffering from shock.' In fact I was the only person in the dining-room who was *not* suffering from shock: I hadn't noticed anything!

Crêpes Suzette

Serves approx. 4.

Pancakes: Put flour in a bowl, make a well in the centre. Into this pour oil, egg, egg yolk and curaçao. Stir, gradually drawing in the flour from the sides as for ordinary pancakes. Add the milk slowly until it is the consistency of thin cream. Leave aside for 30 minutes.

55 g/2 oz/scant½ cup flour
1 tablesp. oil
1 egg
1 egg yolk
2 teasp. orange curaçao
150 ml/¼ pt/⅔ cup milk

Sauce: Grate rind of oranges very carefully so as not to penetrate the white. Add to butter and sugar; cream vigorously until smooth.

225 g/½ lb large ripe oranges
85 g/3 oz/6 tablesp. softened butter
85 g/2 oz/⅜ cup castor sugar

To finish, assemble the following:

frying pan (preferably copper for style)
fondue stove
matches
fork, spoon
orange butter
pancakes
castor sugar
orange curaçao
brandy
hot pudding plates

Put the pan on a flame. Melt about 15 g/½ oz orange butter in it. When bubbling, put the pancake in and heat through on both sides, turning. Fold it into a fan shape. Rest it against the side of the pan. Continue with the remaining pancakes. Sprinkle them with castor sugar. Pour over brandy and curaçao. Set alight, keeping your face away from the flames. Tilt the pan and spoon the juices over the pancakes until the flame subsides. Serve immediately on hot plates.

A Trifling Argument

It's a bit annoying when somebody refers to 'a lady's wine' or 'a man's book'. When it comes to trifle, however, I must admit men, in *particular,* become passionately interested.

I once heard three men arguing about how to make the one-and-only, authentic trifle. Each man's grandmother had made the trifle of his life, and each made it differently.

One of them had a Drogheda granny who made trifle with sponge cakes spread with raspberry jam, topped with tinned pears and moistened with pear juice. These were covered with a layer of custard and another of cream. No decorations, no sherry.

An East Cork granny, belonging to the second man, dissolved jelly in the juice of tinned peaches or pears and poured this with sherry over sponge cakes. She put the fruit between the layers and topped the lot with whipped cream. She used no custard or decorations.

The third man's rather grand Yorkshire granny put ratafia biscuits, macaroons and sponge cakes in layers in the bowl. She moistened them with sherry, fruit juice and lemon curd. Custard and sometimes cream topped the bowl, and crystallised violets and roses were used for decoration.

Well, now I have my own grandsons and this is how I make my trifle — with acknowledgements to my own granny, Harriet Stoker of Cork City. I use Jane Grigson's recipe for pastry cream in place of the usual custard. It comes from her book *Good Things.*

Trifle

Serves approx. 10. Cut cake into pieces 5 x 7.5 cm/2 x 3 in. Spread them with raspberry jam and put them in the bowl. They should come to within 3-4 cm/1½ in of the top. Pour over the sherry. Spread with a thick layer (1-2.5 cm/½-1 in) pastry cream and then a thick layer of whipped cream. Blanch, peel and halve the almonds, halve cherries and cut angelica into little sticks. Decorate the top of the trifle with them. Leave to set for at least 8 hours.

450 g/1 lb sponge cake
450-600 ml/¾-1 pt/2-2½ cups
  pastry cream
225 g/½ lb raspberry jam
175 ml/6 fl oz/¾ cup sherry
600 ml/1 pt/2½ cups whipped
  cream
8 almonds
8 cherries
7 g/¼ oz/8 sticks angelica
1.75 l/3 pt/7½ cup glass bowl

Pastry Cream

For approx. 600 ml/1 pt/2½ cups sauce. Bring milk to the boil with a small piece of vanilla pod in it, or add a few drops of vanilla essence afterwards. Separate the yolks and whites of 2 eggs. Beat the yolks and the whole egg together and pour the boiling milk onto them. Beat in the sugar and sifted flour. Stir over a very low heat, until the custard is thick and cooked. Use a heavy-bottomed saucepan, and be careful to prevent sticking or lumps forming. Strain into a clean bowl. Beat the egg whites stiffly and fold them in. Cool before using.

300 ml/½ pt/1¼ cup milk
vanilla pod or vanilla essence
3 small eggs
110 g/4 oz/½ cup sugar
1 tablesp. hot water
30 g/1 oz/scant ¼ cup flour

Making the Christmas Puddings

The tradition that every member of the household could have a wish which was likely (note, never a firm promise) to come true, was, of course, a ruse to get all the children to help with the heavy work of stirring the pudding. I only discovered this after I was married and had to do the job myself. This recipe, multiplied many times, was made all at once. In a machineless age, mixing all those expensive ingredients properly was a formidable task. Our puddings were mixed in an enormous china crock which held the bread for the household for the rest of the year. My mother, nanny and the cook took it in turns to stir, falling back with much panting and laughing after a few minutes' work. I don't think I was really much help to them.

Christmas puddings should be given at least 6 weeks to mature. They will keep for a year. They become richer and firmer with age, but one loses the lightness of the fruit flavour. We always eat our last plum pudding at Easter.

If possible, prepare your own fresh beef suet — it is better than the pre-packed product.

Plum Pudding

170 g/6 oz/1²/₃ cups shredded
  beef suet
170 g/6 oz/³/₄ cup sugar
900 g/2 lbs loaf/4 cups soft breadcrumbs
225 g/8 oz/1½ cups currants
225 g/8 oz/1½ cups raisins
110 g/4 oz/³/₄ cup candied peel
1-2 teasp. mixed spice
pinch of salt
2 tablesp. flour
3 eggs
60 ml/2 fl oz/¼ cup flesh of
  baked apple
60 ml/2 fl oz/¼ cup whiskey

8-10 helpings. Mix dry ingredients thoroughly. Beat eggs and add them with apple and whiskey. Stir very well indeed. Fill into a greased 1.75 l/3-pint/7½ cup pudding bowl. Cover with a round of greaseproof paper or a butter-wrapper pressed down on top of the pudding. Put a large round of grease-proof or brown paper over the top of the bowl, tying it firmly under the rim. Place in a saucepan one-third full of boiling water and simmer for 10 hours. Do not allow the water to boil over the top and do not let it boil dry either. Store in a cool place until needed.

Boil 1½-2 hours before serving. Left-over pudding can be fried in butter. Serve with Whiskey Cream or Brandy Butter.

Brandy Butter

Soften butter and then beat it until white and creamy with the sugar. Add brandy.

85 g/3 oz/6 tablesp. butter
85 g/3 oz/⅜ cup castor sugar
2 tablesp. brandy

Whiskey Cream

Fold sugar and whiskey into cream

250 ml/8 fl oz/1 cup whipped cream
1 teasp. sugar
1½ tablesp. whiskey

Homemade Candied Peel

Cut the fruit in half and squeeze out the juice. Reserve the juice for another use. Put the peel in a container — not aluminium. Cover with cold water and add salt. Leave to soak for 24 hours. Next day throw away the soaking water, put the peel in a saucepan and cover with fresh cold water. Bring to the boil and simmer very gently until the peel is soft, 3 hours approx. Remove peel and discard water. Scrape out any remaining flesh and membranes from inside the fruit, leaving the white pith and rind intact. Make a syrup by dissolving the sugar in 900 ml/1½ pt/3¾ cups water. Bring to the boil, add peel and simmer gently until it looks translucent, 30 minutes approx.

Remove peel, drain and leave to cool. Boil down the remaining syrup until it becomes thick and white but before it turns to a caramel. Remove from heat and put peel in again to soak up the syrup. Leave for 30 minutes. Remove peel once more, cool on a dish and pour any remaining syrup into the centres. Finally pack into glass jars and cover tightly. It should keep for 6-8 weeks or longer under refrigeration.

5 oranges
5 lemons
5 grapefruit
1 teasp. salt
1.35 kg/3 lbs/6 cups sugar

After Dinner

When times were good, my father brought home Hadji Bey chocolates and the *Illustrated London News* on Saturdays. The chocolates were strictly rationed. They were kept in an unopenable bureau in the diningroom and we got one after dinner each day that they lasted. This all stopped in the 1930s. When I graduated to a bicycle and could rise to two-pence in my pocket, things got better again. I discovered the joy of a stick of Peggy's Leg, and sometimes, even better, Peggy's Toe, from Kelly's in the village.

A sweet with coffee after dinner is a treat at any age, especially if you cut out pudding.

Ballymaloe Chocolates

This is a smaller version of the Iced Chocolate Cases. For approx. 12-14 chocolates. Smear chocolate onto petits fours cases. They should be of double thickness (i.e. one case inside the other). Chill and peel off the paper carefully. It is a good idea to keep some melted chocolate handy for patching, should a crack appear.

Wash, dry and hull strawberries and cut in rounds; or peel and remove pips from grapes. Put fruit in a cup. Pour over syrup and kirsch and leave to soak for 10 minutes approx. Fill the chocolate cases with fruit and pour over the syrup. Serve on a paper doyley within 2 hours.

55 g/2 oz/2 squares softened chocolate
12-14 small strawberries or grapes
6 tablesp. stock syrup
6 tablesp. kirsch

Chocolate Truffles

For approx. 450 g/1 lb chocolates. Crush the praline finely. Melt chocolate over a gentle heat to a thick cream with rum and water. Draw aside; stir in the butter bit by bit, then add the cream and praline. Put out in small teaspoons onto waxed or greaseproof paper.

When set, have ready the melted chocolate. Put a little on the palms of the hands and lightly roll the truffles between them. Toss into a paper of unsweetened chocolate or cocoa powder. Brush off the surplus and put on racks to dry.

170 g/6 oz/6 squares plain chocolate
55 g/2 oz/2 squares unsweetened chocolate
1 tablesp. rum
water
85 g/3 oz/6 tablesp. unsalted butter
2 tablesp. cream
85 g/3 oz/³⁄₄ cup praline
melted chocolate and cocoa for finishing

Strawberries Almandine

For approx. 24 strawberries. Blanch and peel the almonds. Grind them in a liquidiser with the sugar. Cut some of the angelica into little sticks, to resemble strawberry stalks, and put aside until later. Chop the remaining angelica finely and mix it with the almonds and sugar. Moisten the mixture with enough egg white to make a paste.

Wash, dry and hull the strawberries. Sprinkle a board with castor sugar. Take a ball of paste for each strawberry and flatten on the board into a round about 5 cm/2 in across, 3 mm/¹⁄₈ in thick. Place a strawberry in the middle of each and mould the paste around. Cut in half, place the reserved angelica sticks in at one end to resemble stalks and serve in petits fours cases. Serve within 4 hours.

12 strawberries
140 g/5 oz/⁷⁄₈ cup peeled almonds
185 g/6¹⁄₂ oz/³⁄₄ cup approx. castor sugar
2 large egg whites
45 g/1¹⁄₂ oz/¹⁄₂ cup angelica
24 petits fours cases

TIM ALLEN

Useful Sweets

Here are some of the most useful sweets of all. They are inter-changeable: pudding or cake, hot or cold, for a packed lunch, dinner or afternoon tea.

Mince Pies

The mince pies are an old family recipe. The mince meat should be kept for 2 weeks after making. Pot and cover like jam. It should keep for a year in a cool place. Make in November for Christmas. Stir before using. Serve with a sweetened cream flavoured with whiskey or with some whiskey poured through the slit on the top. My mother ate them with a little neat Irish whiskey poured into them; we were always intrigued by the way she carefully measured the whiskey through a fork.

Fruit Tart

Serves approx. 8. Line plate with pastry trimmings or shortcrust rolled into a circle. It should be 7 mm/¼ in thick. Thinly peel and core apples and cut into chunks. Place them in the centre of the pastry leaving a 1 cm/½ in border round the edge. Sprinkle with sugar.

Roll out puff pastry 7 mm/¼ in thick. Cut a circle for the top. Brush the edge of the pastry base with water. Put on the top, press the edges together and knock up the sides. Cut a slit in the centre. Brush with egg wash or egg white. Bake in a moderately-hot oven, 200°C/400°F/Regulo 6, for 30 minutes.

170 g/6 oz puff pastry
170 g/6 oz pastry trimmings
or
shortcrust pastry
450 g/1 lb prepared apples,
gooseberries, plums or
redcurrants
225 g/8 oz/1 cup sugar
25 cm/10 in pie plate

Mince Pies

This recipe fills two 450 g/1 lb jam jars: enough for approx. 30 pies made in shallow 6 cm/2½ in tins.

Put the apple in a hot oven to bake. Grate lemon rind finely without any white pith. Squeeze out the juice. Mix in other ingredients one by one, mixing thoroughly. When the apple is cooked, skin and core it and mix the flesh in thoroughly with the fruit. Put into jam jars and cover closely. Use as required.

1 lemon
1 cooking apple
225 g/8 oz/1½ cups stoned
raisins
110 g/4 oz/¾ cup currants
110 g/4 oz/¾ cup sultanas
55 g/2 oz/⅓ cup candied peel
450 g/1 lb/2 cups firmly-packed,
moist brown sugar
225 g/8 oz/2 cups chopped suet
75 ml/2½ fl oz/generous ¼ cup
whiskey
1 tablesp. orange marmalade

To make up: Roll out pastry very thinly and cut two rounds to fit each tin. Line tins with a round of pastry. Put a heaped teaspoon of mince meat in the centre, wet the edges and press on a pastry lid. Cut a slit in the middle. They can be kept like this for a few days if necessary before baking. Brush with beaten egg before putting in the oven. Bake for 20 minutes approx. in a moderately-hot oven, 200°C/400°F/Regulo 6.

Allow for 12 mince pies:
225 g/½ lb puff or flaky pastry
½-¾ jar mince meat

Apple Cakes

The west coast of Ireland is very bare and completely windswept. The grass is cropped short, burned by the salt winds. Thorn bushes are permanently bent away from the force of the Atlantic gales and trees cannot exist. It is farmed, however, and here and there one finds a farmhouse that accommodates the traveller, offering kindness and hospitality in direct contrast to the severity of the climate.

In one of these farms Mary cooks for three unmarried brothers, their widowed sister and the guests. She never stops working. The house is filled with the smell of her bread, scones, and apple cakes. Opposite is her apple cake recipe. Apple cakes like this one are a traditional sweet in Ireland, and the recipes vary from house to house.

All the apple cakes are made with cooking, not eating, apples. Bramley's Seedlings, the most widely-grown commercial variety at present, break down in the required way to a white foamy mass when cooked. Cut them in chunks. If they are meant to keep their shape as in the Open Apple Tart, they should be sliced.

Irish Apple Cake

Serves approx. 6. Mix flour and baking powder. Rub in the butter with your fingertips until the texture of breadcrumbs. Add 110 g/4 oz/½ cup sugar, beaten egg and enough milk to form a soft dough. Divide in two. Roll one half into a circle to fit a greased ovenproof plate. Peel, core and chop up apples, place them on the dough and add 1 tablespoon sugar. Roll out the remaining pastry and fit on top. Press the sides together, cut a slit through the lid and bake 40 minutes approx., or until cooked through and nicely browned, in a moderate oven, 180°C/250°F/Regulo 4.

225 g/8 oz/1¾ cups flour
¼ teasp. baking powder
110 g/4 oz/½ cup butter
240 g/8½ oz/½ cup and 1 tablesp. sugar
1 egg
120 ml/4 fl oz/½ cup milk approx.
1-2 cooking apples
2-3 cloves (optional)

Open Apple Tart

Approx. 12 tartlets or two open tarts 20 cm/8 in diameter. Line pie plates or patty tins with pastry rolled thinly, about as thick as a coin for tartlets, slightly thicker for tarts. Thinly peel and quarter apples, then cut them into slices 3mm/⅛ in thick, keeping a good even shape. Arrange them on the pastry in overlapping slices. Sprinkle liberally with sugar. Bake 15 minutes approx. in a hot oven, 220°C/425°F/Regulo 7. The juice of the apples will caramelise with the sugar.

225 g/½ lb flaky or puff pastry trimmings
3-4 cooking apples
2 tablesp. sugar approx.

The Apples I Have Loved

My favourite apple tree was about 20 ft high. It had lanky, unpruned, lichen-covered branches and bright red apples. They were tempting to look at, but dreadful to eat. They had one virtue however: they stewed to a beautiful fluffy pink mass. Nobody else liked the tree and one day it was cut down when I was not around to protect it. I have never had pink stewed apple since.

Apples that I love are always disappearing. In mid August we had the red-striped Beauty of Bath — the first delicious eating apple of the season. A fortnight later came creamy Miller's Seedlings, a wonderfully crisp and juicy apple. Next came Worcester Pearmain, bright red and not bad to eat. Laxton's Superb, Cox's Orange Pippin and Russets followed.

On November evenings, my father would select an enormous Charles Ross in perfect condition. Too big for one person, it was solemnly shared between us, as we sat around the fire.

There are hundreds of different varieties of apple, each with its own distinctive characteristics, like the wines of France. Nowadays apple trees, like hens and humans, have to produce with maximum efficiency. The subtler virtues no longer pay.

The recipes opposite will be good made with Golden Delicious, but better with one of the good old-fashioned eating apples.

Apples in Irish Mist

Peel, quarter and cut the apples into 3 mm/⅛ in segments. Put them in a stainless steel or enamel saucepan. Add sugar and the juice of a lemon. Cover the pan tightly and cook on a gentle heat until the apples are soft but not broken. They can be started in the oven, but finish them on top, removing the lid to evaporate the juices. Cool, then stir in liqueur. Use as a filling for open tarts, vol-au-vent or serve with vanilla ice cream.

8 eating apples
170 g/6 oz/¾ cup castor sugar
1 lemon
3 tablesp. Irish Mist

Apple Vol-au-vent

For 12-14 vol-au-vent cases. Roll out the puff pastry 7 mm/¼ in thick. Stamp out into 7.5 cm/3 in rounds. Mark the centre by half cutting with a 4 cm/1½ in cutter. Bake in a very hot oven, 240°C/475°F/Regulo 9, until risen and browned. Cool, remove lids and scrape out the soft pastry from inside.

Stir cream, liqueur and some of the juices from the apple into the pastry cream. Fill the vol-au-vent cases one-half to two-thirds full with this. Fill right up to the top with apple. Put on the pastry lids and dredge heavily with icing sugar.

570 g/1¼ lb puff pastry
450 ml/¾ pt pastry cream
300 ml/½ pt whipped cream
1½ teasp. Irish Mist
Apples in Irish Mist
  (½ recipe)

Jane's Biscuits

The shortcake mixture on the next page makes a good biscuit to go with morning coffee or fruit fools. It was first made for us by one of my children's friends when I decided to let them all loose in the kitchen on a wet Sunday afternoon. No wonder that I so firmly believe in having children in the kitchen, except at certain moments!

Inexpensive Flan

My mother's recipe. I never came across her expensive one. The secret with this is to have crisp pastry. Do not roll too thickly or it will be like cake; nor too thinly or it will be brittle.

They used to be
Jane's biscuits –
now they're mine.

Strawberry Shortcake and Jane's Biscuits

Shortcake:

Serves approx. 6. Rub butter into flour and add sugar, as for shortcrust pastry. Gather the mixture together and knead well. Roll into two circles 17.5 cm/7 in dia. approx., 7 mm/¼ in thick. Bake in a moderate oven, 180°C/350°F/Regulo 4, to pale brown, 15 minutes. Remove and cool on a rack. One circle should be marked with a knife into wedges while still warm, to aid cutting the cake later. Sandwich with sweetened whipped cream and halved strawberries. Sift icing sugar over top.

Biscuits:

Make pastry and roll out as for shortcake. Cut with 6 cm/2½ in round cutter and bake as directed.

170 g/6 oz/1¼ cups flour
110 g/4 oz/1½ cups unsalted butter
55 g/2 oz/¼ cup sugar
225 g/½ lb strawberries
250 ml/8 fl oz/1 cup whipped cream
1 teasp. icing sugar

Rhubarb and Almond Tartlets

Also for grapes, raspberries and fresh peaches. For approx. 16 tartlets. Cut rhubarb into 2.5 cm/1 in lengths and poach in stock syrup until just tender, then drain and cool. Meanwhile beat butter, sugar and almonds together to a cream. Put a teaspoon of the mixture into 16 small patty tins. Bake at 180°C/350°F/Regulo 4 for 10 minutes approx. or until golden brown. Cool in tins but do not allow to set hard before removing to a wire rack. Just before serving place a chunk of rhubarb in each tart, and top with whipped cream. Grapes should be peeled and pipped; peaches should be peeled and sliced.

Almond Tart: This mixture can also be pressed into one 25 cm/10 in or two 15 cm/6 in shallow sandwich tins. Bake and fill as for tartlets.

2 sticks of plump red rhubarb
460 ml/16 fl oz/2 cups stock syrup
85 g/3 oz/6 tablesp. butter
85 g/3 oz/⅜ cup sugar
85 g/3 oz/½ cup ground almonds
300 ml/½ pt/1¼ cups whipped cream

Inexpensive Flan

Rub butter into flour. Add sugar. Moisten with egg. Knead well. Roll out to 7 mm/¼ in thickness. Line a flan ring or shallow tin. Be careful not to have it thick at the corners. Bake to a light brown biscuit colour, approx. 15 minutes. Fill with an apple purée at the last minute before serving.

Note: When baking the flan, line the pastry with soft kitchen paper, and fill up to the top with dried beans or crusts. Bake for 10 minutes or until the pastry is set. Remove this filling and return to the oven to brown. This procedure stops the sides from falling in.

170 g/6 oz/1¼ cups flour
1-2 tablesp. castor sugar
1 egg yolk
1 teasp. egg white
100 g/3½ oz/7 tablesp. butter
500 g/1 lb 2 oz/2 cups sweetened apple purée

Arrivals from Germany

Under the cover of dense fog, a small boat crept out of Hamburg port and down the Elbe on the start of a voyage to South America via Spain. It was August 1948 and on board was a group of Germans seeking a better living in a new land. Some of them had never seen the sea before. They had travelled up some hundreds of miles from Bavaria in the south.

Tremendous gales blew for most of the four weeks of their voyage, forcing them to change their course and make for the Irish coast. They came to a broad estuary, sailed up, tied up at a tiny village pier and waited to be arrested for they had no passports nor permission to leave Germany. Instead, the villagers, incredulous that such a tiny boat could survive such terrible storms, brought presents of food — cheese, bread and a salmon, which they could not cook as their stoves were broken. Eventually, three of them, the Bauer family, found themselves installed on our farm. Unfortunately they had learnt to speak Spanish, not English.

To a family of Irish children, the Bauers might have stepped straight out of a fairy tale. Their hard work and ingenuity was fantastic. For every child's birthday, a plate of Bavarian biscuits decorated with flowers arrived or an adorable hedgehog cake.

Easter brought a hunt for coloured eggs in the garden. Christmas was the most exciting of all. For some weeks before Mr Bauer was known to be working late at night behind the locked door of his workshop. On Christmas morning his masterpiece arrived — a real little house that children could get into, little tin men that chopped wood when the toy was placed over a radiator, or an enormous see-saw.

Every summer Mrs Bauer and her daughter made wines from rhubarb and blackcurrants and in autumn from blackberries, hips and apples. They made sandals and slippers from straw, and a lovely cottage from an old hovel. Opposite is Mrs Bauer's recipe for Bavarian Apple Cake. The German cheese cake in fact is not their recipe, but was picked up by a friend of my daughter on a student visit to Germany.

Bavarian Apple Cake

Approx. 10 slices. Mix flour and baking powder. Rub in the butter with your finger tips until like crumbs. Add sugar. Moisten with an egg to a stiff dough. Roll out and line a shallow 25 cm/10 in sandwich tin or flan ring.

140 g/5 oz/1 cup flour
½ teasp. baking powder
55 g/2 oz/4 tablesp. butter
1 tablesp. sugar
1 egg

Peel and slice apples into the pastry case. Sprinkle with a little extra brown or white sugar if they are bitter. Crumble the butter into the flour and mix in sugar and cinnamon. Sprinkle over the apples. Bake in a moderate oven, 180°C/350°F/Regulo 4, for 45 minutes.

3-4 cooking apples
125 g/4 oz approx./1 scant cup flour
3 level teasp. ground cinnamon
110 g/4 oz/½ cup sugar
70 g/2½ oz/5 tablesp. butter

Cheesecake

Approx. 8 slices. Cut the butter into the flour in little pieces and make like crumbs with the tips of your fingers. Add sugar. Moisten with sufficient egg and water to make a stiff dough. Roll out 7 mm/¼ in thick to line a 18 cm/7 in flan ring.

110 g/4 oz/1 scant cup flour
70 g/2½ oz/5 tablesp. butter
1 tablesp. castor sugar
1 tablesp. beaten egg
2-3 tablesp. water

Separate the egg, sieve cheese and add vanilla essence, yolk, cornflour, 1 tablespoon of sugar, lemon juice and enough milk to soften. Add the currants. Beat the egg white with remaining sugar until stiff. Fold it into the cheese mixture. Fill into a pastry shell and bake in a moderate oven, 180°C/350°F/Regulo 4, for 45 minutes approx. until set.

225 g/8 oz/1 cup cottage cheese
3-4 drops vanilla essence
2 teasp. cornflour
1 egg
2 tablesp. castor sugar
1 teasp. lemon juice
milk as needed
1 tablesp. currants

Childhood Treats

One of the great treats of my childhood was to picnic at a rocky cove on the coast of Cork on a hot summer day. We usually sheltered under the walls of a ruined cottage on a grassy cliff.

My mother would first unpack raw, well-scrubbed potatoes, a saucepan and a spirit stove.

We would bring her a bucket-full of sea water and she would proceed to cook the potatoes in it. In half an hour, we would be wet and shivering from our swim, and ready to do justice to those marvellous potatoes, served with big pats of butter. Cold chicken, ham, brawn and old-fashioned salads of very crisp lettuce with slices of egg and tomato and lashings of salad cream — all appeared out of the picnic basket. Fresh fruit followed.

At 4.30 it was time to find a well and to bring my mother fresh spring water to boil for the tea, while we had our last swim of the day. Tea was taken with freshly-buttered slices of barm brack, perhaps biscuits and cake as well. Then we rumbled home along the dusty roads, we children singing in the back of the car at the tops of our voices. Country girls passed by in brightly-coloured satin dresses, bound for an evening's dancing on the boards at the cross-roads. We begged to stop and wait to see the dancing, but children had to go to bed early — oh dear!

The recipes opposite might suit somebody small, wet and shivery on a windy strand.

Barm Brack

450 g/1 lb/3½ cups flour
pinch of salt
1 teasp. mixed spice
½ oz fresh yeast
1 teasp. sugar
300 ml/½ pt/1¼ cups warm water
85 g/3 oz/6 tablesp. butter
2 eggs
30 g/1 oz/2 tablesp. candied peel
110 g/4 oz/¾ cup raisins
110 g/4 oz/¾ cup sultanas
110 g/4 oz/¾ cup currants
110 g/4 oz/½ cup castor sugar
For Glaze:
2 tablesp. castor sugar
1 teasp. water

Makes two bracks. This recipe will take about three hours to complete. The mixing up, however, does not take long.

Cream the yeast with a teaspoon of sugar. Add water. Sieve flour with salt and spice and mix to a stiff dough with the yeast mixture. Knead until smooth and springy, about 5 mins. Leave this in a bowl covered with a cloth in a warm place for 1 hour or until it has doubled its size.

Now add beaten eggs, fruit, sugar and melted butter. Beat well. Half fill two greased bread tins with the mixture and put back to rise in a warm place, covered with a cloth. Leave for approximately another hour to rise to the top of the tins. Have ready a moderately hot oven, 190°C/375°F/Regulo 6. Bake bracks in this for approximately 50 minutes or until fairly firm and brown.

Dissolve 2 tablespoons of sugar in 4 teaspoons of water over heat, boil for ½ minute, and then brush this glaze over the bracks as they come out of the oven.

Brown Picnic Biscuits

Mix brown and white flours together. Rub in the butter. Add sugar and syrup. Knead and roll out thick. Cut into rectangles and bake in a moderate oven, 160°C/325°F/Regulo 3, for 20 minutes approx. until light brown.

85 g/3 oz/⁵⁄₈ cup approx. brown flour
85 g/3 oz/⁵⁄₈ cup approx. white flour
110 g/4 oz/½ cup butter
1 rounded tablesp. brown sugar
1 rounded tablesp. golden syrup

Brown Fruit Cake

Set your oven at 150°C/300°F/Regulo 2. Cut the butter into several pieces and put it with the treacle in a mixing bowl into the warming oven for 3-5 minutes to soften. Add sugar and beat until soft and fluffy. Add the eggs one at a time and beat in thoroughly. Finally add the fruit, nuts, spice, flour and baking powder, beating well with each addition. Add beer if you find the mixture too stiff. Line and grease the tin and bake for 3-4 hours.

340 g/12 oz/1½ cups butter
1 rounded teasp. treacle
340 g/12 oz/2 cups brown sugar
4 large eggs
340 g/12 oz/3 cups raisins
340 g/12 oz/3 cups sultanas
¼ teasp. cinnamon
110 g/4 oz/1 cup approx. chopped nuts
450 g/1 lb/3½ cups brown flour
1½ teasp. baking powder
120 ml/4 fl oz/½ cup beer

Ginger Snaps

Makes about 50 biscuits. Beat sugar into softened butter. Add egg and beat until light. Beat in treacle, then add sifted dry ingredients and fruit, if used. Beat well again. Grease two large baking sheets and put mixture onto them in teaspoonfuls about 7 cm/3 in apart. Bake in moderate oven, 180°C/350°F/Regulo 4, for approx. 20 mins.

110 g/4 oz/½ cup softened butter
140 g/5 oz/¾ cup brown sugar
1 egg
170 g/6 oz/½ cup treacle (molasses)
255 g/9 oz/1²⁄₃ cup flour
pinch bicarbonate of soda
pinch salt
1 teasp. ground ginger

Optional:
grated rind of 1 orange
5 tablesp. chopped nuts
5 tablesp. raisins

Mrs Lamb's Sponge Cake

Young trainees can make disastrous mistakes. When one occurs, I try to be patient and to remember my own early days when I destroyed so many precious ingredients in war time — fortunately they were my own.

One year I burned three Christmas cakes before I trained myself to take one out of the oven in time.

Another time I beat 16 eggs with their weight in sugar by hand for a whole day, in an effort to achieve the smooth mousse-like texture that I had been taught was the correct basis for a sponge cake. It never happened and the result was finally fed to the chickens. Good came out of this episode in the end, however, when a friend came to my rescue with a much more foolproof recipe.

Baking Bread and Cakes

When you put a loaf of bread or a cake into the oven, you must think of it slowly cooking inwards. As soon as the very centre is just set, it will start a slow process of drying out and deteriorating. So part of the art in baking is to measure and mix correctly, but your success will also depend on judging the exact moment when it is cooked. You will know it is not cooked at first because the centre will move if you shake the tin a little; a little later the centre will be still soft to touch. Finally, the centre is just firm and the cake should come out. Leave it in a tin for 5 minutes, to cool and shrink, then run a knife around the side and turn it out onto your hand, protected with a folded tea-towel and then back the right way on to a cake rack. This system protects the top from getting compressed.

Here are some more tips. The larger the cake, the cooler the oven must be. It is a good idea to have the temperature of the oven a little higher to start with to help the cake to rise. Lower it after about 10 minutes. Put cakes in the centre of the oven. Don't open the oven door for the first half of the cooking period in case the cake falls. Open and close the door gently. Towards the end of the cooking time, it is necessary to open the door and look at the cake more often.

Note: all sponge cakes should be eaten very fresh. They also freeze quite well, even when filled with cream and fruit.

Sponge Cake, Basic Recipe

Separate the eggs. Beat the yolks and sugar for 2 minutes. Blend in water. Whisk until firm and creamy, 10 minutes approx. Fold in sifted flour and baking powder. Beat the egg whites until they hold a stiff peak. Fold them in very gently. Bake in two greased, floured sandwich tins in a moderately-hot oven, 190°C/375°F/Regulo 5, for 20 minutes approx. Fill with whipped cream and fresh fruit and sift icing sugar on top before serving. It is particularly good with blackberries.

3 eggs
90 ml/3 fl oz/⅓ cup water
225 g/8 oz/1 cup sugar
140 g/5 oz/1 cup flour
1 teasp. baking powder

Filling and decoration:
250 ml/8 fl oz/1 cup whipped
  cream
85 g/3 oz/¾ cup fresh fruit
2 teasp. icing sugar

Chocolate Sponge Cake

Make as above, reducing flour by 30 g/1 oz/¼ cup. Add 30 g/1 oz/¼ cup cocoa instead. Sandwich the cake with whipped cream or the following chocolate filling.

Beat butter, sugar and cocoa together. Moisten with hot water to spreading consistency.

Ingredients as above
30 g/1 oz/¼ cup cocoa

140 g/5 oz/1 cup icing sugar
55 g/2 oz/4 tablesp. butter
2 teasp. cocoa

Coffee Sponge Cake

Follow the basic recipe. Dissolve 1 tablespoon of instant coffee in the water and add to the yolks. Fill with whipped cream or the following coffee filling.

Soften butter, beat in sugar and coffee dissolved in hot water.

Ingredients as above
1 tablesp. instant coffee

140 g/5 oz/1 cup icing sugar
55 g/2 oz/4 tablesp. butter
1 teasp. instant coffee
1 teasp. hot water

Coffee Cream Layer Cake

Follow the basic recipe, reducing the flour by 30 g/1 oz/¼ cup and adding 30 g/1 oz/¼ cup cornflour instead. Bake in a square or oblong tin.

Blanch, peel and split the almonds. Cut them into spikes. Have cream ready. When the cake is baked and cool, cut it into four 1 cm/½ in layers, approx. 20 x 12.5 cm/8 x 5 in. Sandwich them together with the filling. Coat the cake with cream and spike with almonds. Whiskey can be added to cream or filling. This cake can also be layered with fresh strawberries, cream and kirsch.

Ingredients as for Mrs Lamb's
  Sponge Cake
30 g/1 oz/¼ cup cornflour

Filling and decoration:
2 tablesp. almonds
460 ml/16 fl oz/2 cups whipped
  cream
coffee filling (2 x recipe above)
whiskey (optional)

Balloons

Balloons are a very cheap and simple doughnut. I sometimes cook them for the children on Sundays. They were a delight in my childhood, when my mother cooked them for me. As she made them, she would share with me her memories of her early married days in Cambridge in the first war; of food queues, old friends I did not know, and bed-sitter parties where a feast was a feed of balloons.

Cynthia

In 1945 the young farmers' clubs of America — the '4H Clubs' — inaugurated the International Farm Youth Exchange scheme (IFYE). They sent young delegates to stay with farming families in Western European countries and took young European farmers back in exchange. These young people are always well informed and skilled in the crafts of the farm and farm home.

In 1955 a young American girl called Cynthia Record came to stay with us under this scheme.

One day she undertook to cook the family lunch. First she gave us the fish 'Baked in Crumbs' and then produced her 'Cocoa Cake' for sweet. Both became standard fare in our household.

Mrs Raymond's Date Cake

Another windfall from America, a speciality of their Agricultural Attaché's wife. (It was well worth going to see *her* at tea time.)

Balloons

140 g/5 oz/1 scant cup flour
2 teasp. castor sugar
pinch of salt
1 level teasp. baking powder
milk
extra castor sugar

Approx. 10 balloons. Sift the dry ingredients into a bowl. Mix to a thick batter (dropping consistency) with milk. Meanwhile, heat fat in a deep fry to 190°C/385°F. Take a dessertspoonful of the mixture and push it gently off with your finger so that it drops in a round ball into the fat. Repeat. Fry until golden. Remove and drain. Roll in castor sugar. Serve at once.

Cynthia's Cake

Approx. 12 slices. Sift the dry ingredients together. Add butter, milk and vanilla essence. Beat for 2 minutes. Add eggs. Beat 2 minutes more. Half-fill three 20 cm/8 in greased sandwich tins. Bake in a moderate oven, 190°C/375°F/Regulo 5, for 30-35 minutes. Tier on top of each other, sandwiched and coated with the following icing:

225 g/8 oz/1¾ cups flour
1 teasp. baking powder
pinch of salt
¼ teasp. bicarbonate of soda
55 g/2 oz/½ cup cocoa
340 g/12 oz/1½ cups sugar
110 g/4 oz/½ cup softened butter
250 ml/8 fl oz/1 cup sour milk
1 teasp. vanilla essence
2 eggs

Icing: Sift sugar and cocoa together. Beat in butter and moisten with coffee to spreading consistency.

285 g/10 oz/2 cups icing sugar
1½ teasp. cocoa
2 teasp. melted butter
coffee as needed

Date and Walnut Cake

Approx. 10 slices. Pour boiling water over the dates and add soda. Cream butter and sugar together and gradually beat in the egg, vanilla essence, flour, baking powder and salt. Finally add walnuts and combine with the date mixture. Bake at 190°C/375°F/Regulo 5 for 35 minutes approx. in a shallow pan 23 x 30 cm/9 x 12 in or two smaller ones. Ice with the following cake frosting and decorate with walnuts.

170 g/6 oz/1 cup chopped dates
250 ml/8 fl oz/1 cup boiling
    water
½ teasp. bicarbonate of soda
225 g/8 oz/1 cup sugar
55 g/2 oz/4 tablesp. softened
    butter
1 beaten egg
1 teasp. vanilla essence
215 g/7½ oz/1½ cups flour
½ teasp. baking powder
pinch of salt
125 g/4½ oz/1 cup chopped
    walnuts
walnuts for decoration

Frosting: Put sugar, cream and butter in a saucepan and boil for 3 minutes. Add icing sugar and cool. Add a little more icing sugar if too liquid.

2½ tablesp. brown sugar
5 tablesp. cream
30 g/1 oz/2 tablesp. butter
45 g/1½ oz/⅓ cup icing sugar
    approx.

Coffee and Chocolate Cakes

The chocolate and coffee cakes are rich and keep up to a week in an air-tight container. Although the coffee essence on sale here has not as good a flavour as an instant coffee, it is thick and sticky and gives the cake a better texture.

Orange Cake

4 eggs
softened butter
sugar
flour
1 teasp. baking powder
2 oranges

Weigh the eggs. Take the same weight in butter, sugar and flour. Beat the butter and sugar together until pale and light in texture. Wash the oranges and add finely-grated rind of 2 and the juice of 1 to the butter mixture. Mix baking powder with flour and add alternately with eggs. Beat thoroughly. Bake in a 24 cm/9½ in tin in a moderate oven, 180°C/350°F/Regulo 4, for 50 minutes approx. Cool the cake, split it in two. Sandwich with half the icing and spread the remainder on top.

Orange Butter Icing

1 orange
110 g/4 oz/½ cup butter
450 g/1 lb/3½ cups icing sugar

Soften the butter. Grate finely the rind of the orange and squeeze out the juice. Beat butter, sugar and orange rind together. Add in enough juice to make the icing of a spreading consistency.

Note: The three cakes above are actually the same recipe. No baking powder is given in the Chocolate Cake. If you put it in, it will lighten the cake a little. It is essential however for the Coffee and Orange Cakes.

The weights are interchangeable. The average egg weighs 55 g/2 oz. It does not matter much whether you actually weigh them, as in the Orange Cake, or presume they will be 55 g/2 oz each, as in the other two cakes. Obviously you make allowances for very big or very small eggs. A Victoria Sponge is the same as this recipe without any flavouring. I have come across a rich Madeira Cake using this recipe also.

Chocolate Cake

Approx. 12 slices. Soften the butter. Beat with the sugar until pale and light in texture. Beat the eggs. Grate the chocolate and mix with flour and cocoa. Add them to the mixture, a little at a time, alternating with additions of beaten egg. Mix in each addition well. Finally add vanilla essence. Turn into a greased, floured 23 cm/9 in tin, the bottom lined with a butter-wrapper cut to fit. Bake until set, 50 minutes approx., in a moderate oven, 180°C/350°F/Regulo 4. Cool the cake and split in two. Sandwich with half the icing and spread the remainder on top.

250 g/8 oz/1 cup softened butter
225 g/8 oz/1 cup sugar
225 g/8 oz/1¾ cups flour
110 g/4 oz/4 squares plain dark
  chocolate
55 g/2 oz/½ cup cocoa
4 eggs
½ teasp. vanilla essence

Chocolate Icing

Melt chocolate in the water. Remove from the heat and beat in the butter and then the eggs, very thoroughly. Leave to cool and set before icing and filling the cake.

170 g/6 oz/6 squares chocolate
2 tablesp. water
55 g/2 oz/4 tablesp. softened
  butter
2 large eggs

Coffee Cake

Approx. 12 slices. Make as for Chocolate Cake, mixing the baking powder with the flour and finally beating in the coffee essence.

225 g/8 oz/1 cup softened butter
225 g/8 oz/1 cup sugar
225 g/8 oz/1¾ cups flour
1 teasp. baking powder
4 eggs
90 ml/3 fl oz/⅓ cup coffee
  essence

Coffee Butter Icing

Sift coffee and icing sugar into a bowl. Melt the butter and beat it in with just enough boiling water to make it of spreading consistency.

110 g/4 oz/½ cup butter
255 g/9 oz/2 cups icing sugar
2 teasp. instant coffee
boiling water

Cakes for Christmas

The first Christmas Cake is rich and moist; it keeps until Easter anyway, I can tell you that, but there my experiment ended!

Make it four to six weeks before Christmas. Keep in a tight tin or a plastic bag in a larder or unheated room until about 12 days before Christmas.

Icing the Cake

Put on the almond icing 12 days before Christmas. Leave it to set for a day before putting on the royal icing, and another day before adding piped decoration. Stuck-on decorations such as fir trees and snowmen are put on immediately, while the icing is soft. The simplest way to control the texture of the icing is in storage. If you keep it in a damp larder it will keep soft — so soft it can run right off the cake in wet weather. If you want it hard and dry, keep it in a warm dry place.

There are several professional ways of rolling and cutting almond pastry to fit a cake. The one I find most fun to do is as follows.

First brush over the top and sides of the cake with a little melted apricot jam or egg white to make it sticky. Sprinkle a pastry board with castor sugar and roll the almond paste out on it into a big circle, put your cake upside down in the middle, block in the edges with spare pieces of paste if it is not already flat and then turn the whole thing over, cake, paste and board, and whoops! The icing is on your cake. Smooth the sides and top flat with a bottle or rolling pin, to meet with a nice sharp right angle.

Christmas Cake

Approx. 20 slices. Blanch, peel and chop the almonds. Grate orange and lemon rinds very finely without any white pith. Cream together the butter and sugar until smooth and white. Add sifted flour and eggs alternately, beating well, then add fruit and other ingredients. Put into a greased and lined tin. Put in an oven, preheated to 160°C/325°F/Regulo 3 for 15 minutes. Reduce to 150°C/300°F/Regulo 2 and bake a further 3 hours approx., watching carefully towards the end.

225 g/8 oz/1 cup softened butter
225 g/8 oz/1 cup sugar
225 g/8 oz/1¾ cups flour
4 eggs
55 g/2 oz/½ cup almonds
90 ml/2½ fl oz/⅓ cup whiskey, rum or brandy
225 g/8 oz/1½ cups currants
225 g/8 oz/1½ cups sultanas
110 g/4 oz/¾ cup raisins
110 g/4 oz/¾ cup glacé cherries
55 g/2 oz/½ cup chopped candied peel
1 lemon
1 orange

Almond Icing

Beat the egg with whiskey and flavouring, add sugar and almonds and work to a stiff paste.

Mild:
225 g/8 oz/1⅓ cups ground almonds
225 g/8 oz/1⅓ cups icing sugar
225 g/8 oz/1 cup castor sugar
1 large egg
squeeze of lemon juice
1 teasp. whiskey

Rich:
340 g/12 oz/2 cups ground almonds
340 g/12 oz/1½ cups castor sugar
1 large egg
few drops of brandy
orange or lemon juice

Royal Icing

Sieve the icing sugar. Whisk the egg whites very slightly, stop before they get frothy. Add them gradually to the sugar, with the lemon juice. Beat very thoroughly until quite white. Keep the icing soft in a bowl covered with a damp cloth, if you do not intend to ice the cake immediately.

450 g/1 lb/3½ cups icing sugar
2 egg whites
2 tablesp. lemon juice approx.

White Christmas Cake

The White Christmas Cake is a small cake, lighter in texture as well as colour. The Chief Gourmet (my husband) prefers it to the first cake. The fruit sinks a little, but we don't mind. The first time I made this cake it went dark. To keep it pale, use a new cake tin and have the oven as clean as possible. Lemon juice whitens it best of all, but a pale whiskey gives it a better flavour.

If you have nothing but red cherries you are in danger of staining your mixture. Your best chance is to keep them whole. A good alternative is to deliberately make a pink Christmas cake. To do this, cut the red cherries into 4 or 5 pieces and colour the icing pink too. It looks very pretty and tastes just as good.

Porter Cake

The Porter Cake is bigger than either of the other two cakes. It is also less expensive. Iced for Christmas, plain at other times of the year, it is a useful recipe. Both these cakes should be made a week or two before Christmas.

White Christmas Cake

Approx. 10 slices. Cream the butter. Add the flour gradually, mixed and sifted with salt and soda. Add lemon juice and whiskey. Beat the egg whites until stiff; fold sugar into them. Mix egg whites with the very stiff cake mixture, a little at a time, until it all comes smooth, white and soft. It seems awful to watch all your carefully beaten white collapsing, but it's alright, it works! Lastly fold in the fruit. Put into a greased, floured tin and bake in a moderate oven, 160°C/325°F/Regulo 3, for 1-1½ hours. Ice as for the previous recipe or with the White Frosting described below.

225 g/8 oz/1⅔ cups flour
125 g/4½ oz/9 tablesp. butter
285 g/10 oz/1¼ cups castor sugar
100 g/3½ oz/⅔ cup halved
    green or yellow cherries
70 g/2½ oz/½ cup shredded
    almonds
55 g/2 oz/½ cup shredded peel
pinch of salt
scant ¼ teasp. bicarbonate of soda
6 egg whites
1¼ teasp. lemon juice
1 teasp. whiskey

White Frosting

Dissolve sugar, cream of tartar and baking powder in water and bring to the boil, stirring to prevent burning. Whisk the egg white with salt until stiff and gradually add the syrup, continuing to whisk. When half is in, add the lemon juice. Add the remaining syrup. Sit the bowl on a saucepan of boiling water and continue whisking until the icing is stiff enough to go on the cake. Ice the cake straight away.

225 g/8 oz/1 cup sugar
1 egg white
1 tablesp. lemon juice
60 ml/2 fl oz/¼ cup water
pinch of baking powder
pinch of cream of tartar
pinch of salt

Porter Cake

Cream butter and sugar. Add sieved flour and beaten eggs alternately. Beat well for 20 minutes. Add the remainder of the ingredients. Dissolve the soda in porter and add it lastly. Bake as directed for Christmas Cake.

450 g/1 lb/3½ cups flour
340 g /12 oz/1½ cups well-
    packed brown sugar
225 g/8 oz/1 cup butter
4 eggs
1 teasp. mixed spice
300 g/10 oz/2 cups approx.
    raisins
300 g/10 oz/2 cups approx.
    sultanas
150 g/5 oz/1 cup approx. currants
110g/4 oz/½ cup chopped peel
90 ml/2½ fl oz/⅓ cup porter
1 teasp. bicarbonate of soda

Organisation

Ballymaloe has always been too big for us to live in as a family home. During the first 20 years here, we had it divided in two with a succession of tenants living in the south wing. Once a young American technician arrived for some months with a very elegant wife and four small children. Every evening when the husband arrived home, the children were in bed and the wife prettily dressed sitting in the evening sun with drinks ready and his dinner, of at least three courses, keeping warm.

At that moment my children were all still milling around and the most I could get on the table was some brown bread and scrambled eggs.

Oh, I was envious! What a dream she had achieved. On looking closer into the organisation, however, I finally decided that whatever one's strength and determination in quelling the children, good brown bread and butter and a free-range egg were, in fact, preferable in every way to a 3 course canned meal.

Waiter – there's some chaos in my soup.

Ballymaloe Brown Bread

When making this bread, remember that yeast is a living fungus. In order to grow, it requires warmth, moisture and nourishment. The growing process produces carbon dioxide which makes the bread rise. Hot water will kill yeast. Have the ingredients and equipment at blood heat. The yeast will rise on sugar or treacle. We use treacle. The dough rises more rapidly with 110 g/4 oz yeast than with only 55 g/2 oz. The flour we use is wholemeal, stone ground. Different flours produce breads of different textures. The amount of natural moisture in flour varies according to atmospheric conditions. The quantity of water should be altered accordingly. The dough should be just too wet to knead. In fact it does not require kneading. The main ingredients, wholemeal flour, treacle and yeast, are highly nutritious.

Mix flour with salt and warm it (in the cool oven of an Aga or Esse or in the electric or gas oven when starting to heat). Mix treacle with some of the water in a small bowl and crumble in the yeast. Put the bowl in a warm position such as the back of the cooker. Grease bread tins and put them to warm, also warm a clean tea-towel. Look to see if the yeast is rising. It will take 5 minutes approx. to do so and will have a frothy appearance on top. Stir it well and pour it with remaining water into the flour to make a wettish dough. Put the mixture into the greased, warmed tins and put the tins back in the same position as used previously to raise the yeast. Put the tea-towel over the tins. In 20 minutes approx. the loaves will have risen by twice their original size. Now bake them in a hot oven, 230°C/ 470°F/Regulo 8, for 45-50 minutes or until they look nicely browned and sound hollow when tapped. Dried yeast may be used instead of baker's yeast. Follow the same method but use only half the weight as given for fresh yeast. Allow longer to rise.

This is our version of 'The Grant Loaf' (Doris Grant, *Our Daily Bread*, Faber and Faber). American measures as given by James Beard.

For four loaves
(13 cm x 20 cm/5 in x 8 in
  approx.)
1½ kg/3½ lb wholemeal flour
1¼ l/2¼ pt water at blood heat
1 tablesp. salt
1-2 well rounded teasp. black
  treacle
2-4 oz yeast

For one loaf
(13 cm x 20 cm/5 in x 8 in
  approx.)
450 g/1 lb wholemeal flour
350 ml/12 oz water at blood heat
1 teasp. black treacle
2 teasp. salt
30 g/1 oz yeast

For one loaf
(American measures)
(13 cm x 20 cm/5 in x 8 in
  approx.)
3¾ cups whole wheat flour
1½ cups (or more) warm water
1½ packages granular yeast
2 tablesp. molasses
salt

Kneading

I was many years married before I first triumphantly put a really good brown soda loaf on the tea table. Of course, this brought me no praise, only a few disillusioned grunts about the pity it was that I had taken so long to learn the art!

Yeast bread, cakes, pastry — anything had been to me easier than the elusive national loaf. Every woman I knew who made good bread appeared just to have 'the touch' — some swore by kneading, others by never kneading, some put in half white flour, some none, and of course, nobody ever went by standard measures — neither did I in the end. Discovering the exact quantities I really use instead of the magic guess resulted in several bad loaves before I succeeded in measuring my best guess.

Making Soda Bread

Bread soda (bicarbonate of soda) and kneading are two of the factors which influence the texture of the bread. There is a thin line between having enough soda to raise the flour and not so much that the flavour and colour are affected. Decreasing the proportion of brown flour helps one to achieve a better loaf. Heavy kneading with too dry a dough results in too close and 'heavy' a loaf. Have the dough wet enough to bend and fold easily with a light touch and cease to knead when it becomes stiff. No kneading at all is much better than heavy kneading. Soda scones are made in the same way as soda bread.

If sour milk is not available, substitute sweet milk and use baking powder instead of bread soda. A mixture of sweet and sour milk with a mixture of bread soda and either cream of tartar or baking powder can make an excellent loaf. Use the full amount of bread soda as is called for in the recipe plus half that quantity in cream of tartar or baking powder. At least, such a mixture has worked like magic for me after struggling with a succession of sluggish loaves.

Sour cream can replace some or all of the butter enrichment and some of the milk.

Irish Brown Soda Bread

Mix dry ingredients very well. Moisten with sour milk. Knead lightly. Form into a round, mark with a cross and bake 30-45 minutes in a fairly hot oven. Buttermilk or whey are excellent substitutes for sour milk.

620 g/1lb 6 oz/4 cups wholemeal flour
140 g/5 oz/1 cup white flour
55 g/2 oz/scant ½ cup oatmeal
1 teasp. bicarbonate of soda
1 teasp. salt
470-720 ml/16-24 fl oz/2-3 cups sour milk

Scones

For 12 scones. Sieve flour, salt and soda together into a large bowl. Cut in fat and rub in until like crumbs. Add sugar and enough milk to make a soft dough together with a beaten egg if used. Turn onto a floured board, lightly knead a few times, roll out and cut into round 'cakes' 2.5 x 5 cm/1 x 2 in approx., or diamonds of about the same size. Bake in a hot oven, 200°C/400°F/Regulo 7, for 15 minutes approx. until risen and nicely browned.

285 g/10 oz/2 cups flour
pinch of salt
¼ teasp. bicarbonate of soda
55 g/2 oz/4 tablesp. butter
1 tablesp. sugar (optional)
250 ml/8 fl oz/1 cup sour milk approx.
1 egg (optional)

Sultana Scones

Add sugar to the basic recipe and 1-2 tablespoons of sultanas.

Brown Scones

Make with half brown and half white flour. Quantities and method as above.

Brown Cheese Biscuits

For approx. 16 biscuits. Mix flours, salt and baking powder together. Rub in butter. Moisten with cream and enough water to make a firm dough. Roll out 3 mm/⅛ inch thick approx. Cut with a 2 in round cutter. Prick. Bake at 180°C/350°F/Regulo 4 until lightly browned.

110 g/4 oz/1 cup brown flour
110 g/4 oz/1 cup white flour
½ teasp. baking powder
½ teasp. salt
30 g/1 oz/2 tablesp. butter
1 tablesp. cream
water as needed

White Yeast Bread

The village bakery was still operating in Cloyne up to 1975. We often drove in to collect a few hot crusty loaves for breakfast at Ballymaloe. Then one day the baker did not arrive for work, and that was the end of the bakery.

Baking was a family trade, handed down from father to son. I used to be scornful of this. I could grill steaks, make soup, puddings and cakes — why so much fuss about one operation, just bread? Having tried to teach bread-making to many young cooks since then, I now understand that experience counts for much. The moisture content of the flour varies with the weather and determines how much water should be added. The temperature of the mixture, the amount it should rise, the effect of putting so many loaves into so big an oven at such and such a temperature: all affect the finished loaf. Brown bread is more difficult than white.

Without our village bakery, we started to make our own white bread. Everybody loves it. It is a recipe from the Department of Education publication, *Cooking for All.* We usually make half our mixture into loaves and half into plaits. We crisp up the plaits in a hot oven before serving.

White Soda Bread

The recipe opposite is sometimes made with the addition of sultanas. This was known as 'Spotted Dog' in my childhood. All through the first half of this century, it was common to find it made with the addition of yellow (pronounced 'yaller') meal. This was maize meal and was the last relic of Famine cooking.

If you use too much soda, the bread will taste of it and have a yellowish appearance — if you use too little, the bread will not rise properly. If you cannot get sour milk, you can either use yoghurt, acidulate fresh milk with lemon, or use fresh milk and replace the bicarbonate of soda with baking powder.

White Yeast Bread

For two 450 g/1 lb loaves. Blend yeast with 150 ml/¼ pt/⅝ cup lukewarm water. Put the butter, salt and sugar into a bowl with 300 ml/½ pt/1¼ cup hot water. Stir until sugar is dissolved and butter is melted. Cool to blood heat and combine with yeast. Stir the mixture into the flour and mix well to a loose dough, adding more flour or water as is necessary. Turn the dough onto a floured board, cover and leave to relax for 10 minutes. Knead until smooth and put to rise. Knock back and leave to relax for a further 10 minutes. Divide in two and put in greased tins, or make a plait. Cover and allow to rise to double its size, 20-30 minutes approx. It is ready for baking when a small dent remains if pressed lightly with the finger. Bake in a hot oven, 230°C/450°F/Regulo 9, 30-35 minutes approx.

680 g/1½ lbs/5¼ cups strong
   flour
20 g/¾ oz fresh yeast
2 level teasp. salt
15 g/½ oz/1 tablesp. sugar
30 g/1 oz/2 tablesp. butter
450 ml/¾ pt/2 cups water, more
   as needed

White Soda Bread (basic recipe)

Sift the dry ingredients together. Make a well in the centre. Pour in the milk gradually, mixing in the flour from the sides. Don't have the mixture too dry. Turn it out on a floured board, knead lightly for a few minutes. Pat the dough to a flat cake 5 cm/2 in high approx., and cut a cross on it. Brush it with milk and bake in a hot oven, 230°C/450°F/Regulo 7-8, for 30-45 minutes.

If you have any doubts about the 'doneness', tap the bottom of the cake. If it sounds hollow, it is cooked.

450 g/1 lb/3½ cups flour
½ teasp. sugar
½ teasp. salt
½ teasp. bicarbonate of soda
300-600 ml/½-1 pt/1¼-2½ cups
   sour milk or buttermilk
   to mix

Hot Cross Buns

Warm the milk to blood heat. Sift together the flour, salt and spice. Rub in butter and add 2 tablespoons castor sugar, currants and sultanas. Cream yeast with 1 teaspoon sugar. Beat an egg and blend it with yeast. Make a well in the centre of the dry mixture; add in the yeast, egg and enough milk to make a soft dough. It should be dry enough to knead however. Leave it in a warm place, covered with a clean cloth, to rise to double its size. This will take 1½ hours approx.

Meanwhile roll out the pastry and cut it into strips for the crosses, 5 cm x 7 mm/2 x ⅜ in approx. Make a glaze by dissolving 1 tablespoon sugar in 1 tablespoon milk. When the dough has risen, knock it down, knead it lightly and divide it into 16 pieces. Shape each into a round cake 5 x 2.5 cm/2 x 1 in high. Brush with the glaze. Put a pastry cross on top. Place on a greased baking sheet. Cover with the warm tea-towel and leave in a warm position, such as over a cooker or radiator, to rise again, 20 minutes approx. Bake in a hot oven, 230°C/450°F/Regulo 9, for 15 minutes approx.

300 ml/½ pt/1¼ cups milk
450 g/1 lb/3½ cups flour
½ teasp. salt
2 teasp. mixed spice
55 g/2 oz/4 tablesp. butter
2 tablesp. castor sugar
85 g/3 oz/¾ cup currants
85 g/3 oz/¾ cup sultanas
15 g/½ oz yeast
1 teasp. and 1 tablesp. sugar
1 egg
300 ml/½ pt/1½ cups warm milk
   approx.
1 tablesp. milk

Make a Chest of Sandwiches

A 2 lb loaf makes approx. 16 afternoon tea sized sandwiches. Take a pan or a cottage loaf, and a long sharp bread knife.

Insert the knife at the side just over the bottom crust, just inside the back of the loaf. Push it through until it reaches, but does not go through, the crust on the far side. Without making any bigger the cut through which the knife was inserted, work the knife in a fan shape as far forward as possible, then pull it out. Do the same from the opposite corner at the other end of the loaf. The bread should now be cut away from the bottom crust inside without a noticeable mark on the exterior of the loaf.

Next cut through the top of the loaf to make a lid, carefully leaving one long side uncut, as a hinge.

Finally, with the lid open, cut the bread away from the sides. Ease it carefully, it should turn out in a solid brick leaving an empty case behind.

Cut it into slices, long horizontal ones, or square vertical ones, it does not matter, but stack them, butter them and fill them carefully in the order in which they were cut. Press them together firmly and fill them back, still in order into the loaf.

For a picnic: Close the top of the case and wrap it up. It will keep the sandwiches very fresh.

For a party: Leave the lid slightly open. Decorate inside and out with lettuce and watercress leaves, small ripe tomatoes, spring onions etc. to look like a little hamper overflowing with fruit and vegetables.

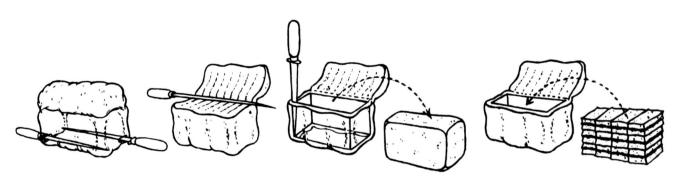

TIM ALLEN

Chef Roland

In the 1960s, the most prestigious kitchen in Ireland was that of the Russell Hotel in Dublin under Chef Roland. Many of our best chefs today spent some time training under him.

One day I decided to ask the manager if my eldest daughter, Wendy, would be accepted in the kitchen for a few months. He was doubtful. A girl had never entered their kitchen (except to clean up after the men); however, he would ask the chef. The message came back that in fact he would love to have a girl in the kitchen — particularly as she already had learned to cook in France, so off she went. Wendy brought home a great many good tips. One saying of Mr Roland was 'If you cannot get your dish right, just add more butter or cream.'

When I started to make chicken liver pâté, I followed this advice — using plenty of butter in this case.

The Danish Expedition

Many years ago, when we started a herd of Jerseys, we went on an unsuccessful expedition to Denmark. We wanted to buy a Danish Jersey bull to increase the butterfat content of our milk.

It transpired, in the end, that we would not be permitted to import one of these fine Danish bulls, but we spent a pleasant week looking at their herds. We drank homemade wines in spotless farmhouse parlours, met sweet, flaxen children and thought that even their pigs had a quieter temperament than ours.

We did not come home quite empty handed, either. I was armed with this recipe for Danish liver paste which I have made ever since, whenever we kill a pig.

Pâté Maison

Fry the chicken livers in some of the butter. Rub through a sieve. Boil and scrape out the pan with brandy. Mix with the livers. Beat in the remaining butter, garlic and thyme. Season carefully. Put in small pots and run melted butter over the top.

110 g/4 oz chicken livers
1 tablesp. brandy
85 g/3 oz/6 tablesp. butter
½ teasp. thyme leaves
1 large clove garlic
butter for topping
salt and pepper

Danish Liver Paste

Mince the liver, fat and onions. Melt the butter, stir in flour, salt and milk. Remove from heat and add egg yolks. Mix with the meat and liquidise. If no liquidiser is available, the meat should be put through a mincer 3 times. Beat the egg whites stiffly and fold into the mixture. Fry a little on a pan to taste for seasoning. More salt should be added if pork fat is used. Bake 1½ hours approx. in a pan half-filled with water, in a moderate oven. This keeps well, but the flavour is best when freshly cooked. It can also be cut in slices and fried.

500 g/18 oz pork liver
500 g/18 oz pork or bacon fat
2 onions
110 g/4 oz/½ cup butter
6 egg yolks
6 egg whites
110 g/4 oz/1 scant cup
   wholemeal flour
1 level tablesp. salt approx.

Turnovers

Hard little bits of Stilton close to the rind, strong, yellowed scraps of Brie or Camembert, and all the left-over ends of good table cheeses that nobody wants to eat will make delicious turnovers for a snack or picnic.

Some of my best
turnovers
are from
left overs

Cheese Turnovers

Makes approx. 12 turnovers. Bring milk to boil with herbs and vegetables. Simmer 5-10 minutes. Remove herbs and vegetables and crumble roux. Reboil, whisking.

Remove rinds and mould if present on cheese. Grate finely. Mix with sauce. Roll pastry out thinly. Cut into rounds 10 cm/4 in dia. Put 1-2 teaspoons of mixture in the centre, leaving a border round the edge. Brush border with egg wash, fold in two and crimp the edges together tightly. Cut a hole in the top, brush over with more egg wash and bake in a hot oven, 200°C/400°F/Regulo 6 for 20 minutes approx.

Egg Wash: Use left-over egg white or egg beaten with ¼ teaspoon salt.

250 ml/8 fl oz/1 cup milk
parsley stalks
sprig of thyme
slice of onion
slice of carrot
60 g/2 oz/¼ cup roux
170 g/6 oz/¾ cup grated cheese
225 g/8 oz puff pastry
egg wash

Dutch Cheese Croquettes

Makes approx. 12. Make a thick white sauce with milk and roux. Stir in yolks, cheese and chives. Cool. Shape into croquettes, dip in flour, brush with beaten egg and roll in toasted breadcrumbs. Chill until very solid. These are best deep fried, but can also be fried in shallow fat.

225 g/8 oz/1 cup roux
450 ml/15 fl oz/scant 2 cups milk
2 egg yolks
225 g/8 oz/2½ cups grated
  cheddar cheese
1 heaped tablesp. chopped chives
salt and pepper
seasoned flour
1 beaten egg
dried breadcrumbs

Ballymaloe Cheese Fondue

Put ingredients into a small saucepan or fondue pot. Heat until bubbling. Serve immediately with fresh French bread or cubes of ordinary white bread crisped up in the oven.

Allow per person:
1 tablesp. dry white wine
½ small crushed clove garlic
1 teasp. tomato chutney
1 teasp. chopped parsley
85 g/3 oz/1 cup grated cheddar
  cheese
bread

Johnny

Johnny is American. He has eaten in every top restaurant in Europe and has often penetrated their kitchens as well. As a carroty-haired teenager, he greatly preferred life on our farm during the long summer holidays. He was always worth consulting over food. 'What do you think of my pizza?' I risked asking him. 'Well,' he drawled, struggling to be polite, 'I can't say it's the *best* pizza I ever had.' So I went back to the kitchen to try again. After endless experiments, this recipe has evolved as the one for *us* and draws more favourable comments.

Pizza

Serves approx. 8. Sieve flour with salt and make a well in the centre. Dissolve yeast in water and turn into well. Work flour gradually into centre and knead for several minutes. Add oil. Knead 10 minutes approx. or until the dough becomes springy. Cover with a cloth, leave for 1 hour in a warm place to rise to double its bulk. Punch it down and roll or stretch into a 7 mm/¼ in thick round, 28 cm/11 in dia. approx., leaving it thicker at the edges. Cover and rise again for ½-1 hour more or until the dough has doubled in bulk again.

900 g/2 lbs very ripe tomatoes
450 g/1 lb onions
45 g/1½ oz/3 tablesp. butter or
* oil*
45 g/1½ oz/½ cup grated
* cheddar cheese*
or
30 g/1 oz approx./¼ cup Gruyère
* cheese*
6-8 black olives
small tin anchovies
½ teasp. finely-chopped rosemary
salt and pepper
½ teasp. sugar

Meanwhile make the topping.

Peel and seed the tomatoes, and chop them roughly. Peel, slice and sauté the onions until soft, in butter or oil. Cook the tomatoes down to a fairly dry purée, seasoning them with a sprinkle of salt, freshly-ground black pepper and a little sugar.

When the dough has risen for the second time, spread it with the cooked onions, leaving 1 cm/½ in rim clear at end. Cover the onions with the grated cheese and then the tomato purée. Decorate the top with anchovy strips and halved, stoned olives. Sprinkle with rosemary. Bake for 30 minutes approx. in a hot oven, 200°C/400°F/Regulo 7.

255 g/9 oz/1¾ cups flour
½ teasp. salt
30 g/1 oz yeast
120 ml/4 fl oz/½ cup tepid water
1 tablesp. oil

Macaroni Cheese

Bring 2.25 l/4 pts/10 cups water with 2 teaspoons salt to the boil. Put in macaroni and cook until just soft, 15 minutes approx. Meanwhile melt butter and cook onions gently in it until soft. Stir in the flour and cook, stirring occasionally for 2 minutes. Blend in the milk and reboil, keep stirring. Add parsley, salt and pepper to taste, and 350 ml/½ pt/1¼ cups cheese. Stir in macaroni and turn into a pie dish. Sprinkle top with remaining cheese. Reheat in hot oven until top is browned.

Good served with cold meat, particularly ham.

225 g/8 oz/2 cups macaroni
2.25 l/4 pts/10 cups water
salt
110 g/4 oz/1 cup chopped onion
* or spring onion including*
* green stalks*
45 g/1½ oz/3 tablesp. butter
2 tablesp. flour
600 ml/1 pt/2½ cups boiling milk
170 g/6 oz/2 cups grated cheese

Egg Recipes

Here are some egg recipes. The hot one is to be made quickly and eaten immediately; the other, cold, can be prepared in advance and left ready.

When six children and a husband are all waiting for their supper together, you can't start making individual omelettes or a riot will ensue. I solved the problem by making just one big one. When we entertained our Danish friend with our family omelette one day, he said excitedly, 'Oh, Flaeskeaeggekage. We have exactly this in Denmark.'

'So, bang goes yet another of my original recipes,' I thought. It was not so, however. The Danish Flaeskeaeggekage has flour in it; it is more like a pancake and is baked in the oven.

Oeufs Argenteuil

6 slices buttered toast
6 eggs
300 ml/½ pt/1¼ cups
  Hollandaise sauce
225 g/8 oz asparagus

Serves 6. Boil the asparagus in salted water until soft. Put soft-boiled eggs on toast, surrounded with well-drained asparagus and coated with sauce. Serve immediately.

Oeufs Benedictine

6 eggs
6 fried croûtons
55 g/2 oz cooked ham
300 ml/½ pt/1¼ cups Béarnaise
  sauce

Serves 6. The croûtons should be cut to fit the eggs. Cut the cooked ham to fit the croûtons, warm the ham a little and put on the croûtons. Surmount the ham with the soft-boiled eggs and coat with Béarnaise sauce. Serve immediately.

Oeufs Beau Rivage

6 eggs
6 fried croûtons
55 g/3 oz smoked salmon
300 ml/½ pt/1¼ cups
  Hollandaise sauce

Serves 6. Make exactly as for Oeufs Benedictine, substituting smoked salmon for ham. Finish by browning under a grill.

Eggs with Tomato and Cheese

6 eggs
6 slices bread, 5 x 10 cm/2 x 4 in
  approx.
350 ml/12 fl oz/1½ cups tomato
  fondue
350 ml/12 fl oz/1½ cups cheese
  sauce
1 tablesp. grated cheese

Serves 6. Toast and butter the slices of bread, or fry them until crisp. Put onto each piece a tablespoon of hot fondue, a soft-boiled egg and a coating of cheese sauce. Sprinkle with grated cheese and brown under a grill. Serve immediately.

Ingredients as above
Substitute creamed spinach for
  tomato fondue

Oeufs Florentine
Make as above.

Family Omelette

Serves approx. 4. Put the eggs, water and seasoning in a large bowl. Whisk for 5 minutes approx. or until the eggs froth up to 3 or 4 times their original bulk. Meanwhile, heat the butter in a large pan. Just before it turns brown, pour in the egg mixture. Reduce the heat. When the bottom is set, sprinkle in the filling; it will sink through the frothy top. Remove from heat when still slightly runny under froth. Do not fold. Serve in segments straight from the pan.

¼ teasp. butter
6 eggs
60 ml/2 fl oz/¼ cup water
salt and pepper
2 tablesp. chopped ham
1 tablesp. parsley
1 tablesp. chopped chives

Chutneyed Eggs

Serves 6. Hard boil eggs, peel and cut in half. Sieve the yolks with the chutney, beat in the softened butter. Fill into a forcing bag fitted with a 2.5 cm/1 in star nozzle. Pipe a rosette into each egg white. They may be decorated with a round slice cut from a gherkin, stuck on top like a sail.
Serve with any of the cold vegetable salads mentioned already.

6 eggs
1 tablesp. chutney
55 g/2 oz/4 tablesp. butter
1 gherkin (optional)

Oeufs Mollet (boiled eggs)

'Molly' eggs was the term used in my kitchen. Quickly made, they can be dressed up to kill, will do for a children's tea party or to start a dinner party. They are a better shape than poached eggs which can be used instead, but they take more careful timing. The yolk must be still soft, the whites well set or they will break. They can be peeled and kept in hot water while the garnish is being prepared.
Boil eggs for 4-5 minutes. Meanwhile cut oval croûtons of bread rather bigger than the eggs and fry them in a good fat until golden. Use butter, oil, bacon fat or fresh beef dripping in order of preference and according to what will go on top. Peel the eggs, set them on the croûtons and spoon over the sauce. The following recipes are for eggs prepared in this way.

6 eggs
3 slices white bread
frying fat

Eggs with Hot Herbed Mayonnaise

Make a sauce with one soft-boiled yolk, oil and lemon juice as for mayonnaise. Add hot stock and other ingredients and chopped egg white. Place bowl over a saucepan of boiling water and stir until it thickens to coating consistency. Prepare eggs as above, spoon over the sauce and serve immediately.

Ingredients as above
120 ml/4 fl oz/½ cup oil
¼ teasp. French mustard
¼ teasp. salt
2 teasp. lemon juice
2 teasp. finely-chopped shallots or spring onions
2 teasp. chopped herbs
60-120 ml/2-4 fl oz/¼-½ cup stock

Some Drinks

TIM ALLEN

The Priest's Table

'We had two fine fat trout that were sweet too, and substantial. One of them as large as a small salmon. Then followed hard boiled hen eggs and bruised asparagus, swimming in butter, laid out on fresh whipped cream and salt. Port wine and scaltin to drink.'

The above is from an account of a Kilkenny school teacher dining with the parish priest, a Fr Heneberry, in the last century. It is translated from Irish.

Another dinner consisted of three dishes: 'Beef tripe swimming in butter and fresh milk, bacon with beef kidneys and white cabbage, roast duck with green peas, scalteen to drink.'

That hospitable gourmet, Fr Heneberry, entertained four guests on yet another occasion, this time the fare was:

'. . . boiled leg of mutton with carrots and turnips. A roast goose with green peas and stuffing followed. Then came a dish of tripe cooked in fresh milk. To drink we had port wine and scalteen.' *(Lin Lae a Mhaoibh* by Tomás de Bháldraithe)

From these accounts one might suspect that provincial Ireland once ate almost as well as provincial France.

After all that food and port wine, the scalteen must have afforded a sweet soporific pudding and drink combined: a comforting way to end a meal after a strenuous day.

Cure for a Sore Throat

The Carrageen drink is for anyone suffering from an extremely sore throat, tonsilitis or measles. Sips of it provide a velvety healing potion to assuage the pain. Only offer it to severe cases or you will not be thanked for what is in other circumstances an unattractive drink.

The two citrus drinks are mush more acceptable in health or minor illnesses, and can be laced with gin, rum or whiskey.

Punch

A delicious, warming drink. It just possibly *could* cure a cold! Many people are sure it does! It is certainly cheering for one facing such a prospect. Take at night, before getting into a warm bed.

Scalteen

Blend whiskey and honey together and stir in hot milk.

Allow per person:
1 teasp. honey
30 ml/1 fl oz/⅛ cup whiskey
140 ml/¼ pt/⅝ cup hot milk

Carrageen Throat Syrup

Soak carrageen for 10 minutes in cup of water. Remove and put in 300 ml/½ pt/1¼ cups fresh cold water and bring to the boil slowly. Strain and add honey and lemon juice to taste. The drink should be thick and syrupy.

120 ml/2 fl oz/¼ cup carrageen
600 ml/1 pt/2½ cups water
* approx.*
2-4 teasp. honey
½ lemon

Stock Syrup

Dissolve the sugar in water and boil together for 2 minutes. Store in a covered jar in the refrigerator until needed.

450 g/1 lb/2 cups sugar
600 ml/1 pt/2½ cups water

Lemonade

Squeeze the juice from the fruit and mix with syrup and water to taste.

2 lemons
1 orange
250 ml/8 fl oz/1 cup syrup
* approx.*
750 ml/1¼ pt/3 cups water
* approx.*

Citrus Drink

Make as for Lemonade. A little more syrup and water may be necessary.

1 orange
1 lemon
1 grapefruit

Punch

Take a tall glass for each person. Put in whiskey, lemon stuck with cloves, and sugar. Fill to the top with boiling water.

Allow per person:
75 ml/2½ fl oz/¼ cup Irish
* whiskey*
1 thick slice of lemon
10-12 cloves
2 teasp. sugar

What goes with What:

Some people know exactly how, when and with what, they wish to serve any dish that takes their fancy. Others are less sure. For the latter I give a very rough guide to wine, drinks and vegetable accompaniments for fish, meat, savouries and sweets.

Wines

By some strange miracle, or perhaps by a slow process of evolution and the discrimination of generations of growers, the wines of the various districts of France in particular, of Germany, of Italy and I'm sure of other countries too, go perfectly with the food of the area in which they are produced. This is worth remembering.

Fish requires a dry white wine. If you buy a bottle from the Loire district or Bordeaux in the west of France, you will not go far wrong.

Pork is eaten a lot in Alsace and in Germany. Try a Rhine wine or a white or Rosé from Alsace. The wine need not be too dry.

Chickens and Turkeys are eaten everywhere and go with a wide range of wines. They can be red or white, dry or semi-dry, a German, a red Bordeaux (known as claret) or a white Burgundy, are three suggestions that would be acceptable.

Lamb needs a slightly drier wine. A red Bordeaux would be very safe.

Duck, Goose and Beef are rich and would go well with a red Burgundy.

Egg and Cheese dishes and Pâtés go well with any dry or medium dry, red or white wine, in fact any wine that is not too sweet.

If you use wine in the cooking of a dish, drink the same sort of wine when eating it.

Curries do not go with wine. Spices grow outside the wine belt. Try a fresh lime and soda instead.

Vegetable and other Accompaniments

Vegetables: All fish dishes go well with green salad, but not with many other vegetables.

Grilled and fried fish go well with fried potatoes. The small thin chips, Pommes Alumettes (matchstick potatoes), are nicest. Green Salad is by far the best accompaniment.

Baked and poached fish go with crisp fresh bread, toast or oven-baked toast (bread cut in inch-thick slices and then divided again into three or four thick pieces and baked until brown and crisp in a hot oven). Boiled potatoes soaked in parsley butter would be most suitable, or Pomme Mousseleine, which is a soft purée of potato with a great deal of milk whisked in. Buttered cucumbers or sautéd mushrooms are delicious. One can also serve creamed spinach, buttered leeks, tomato fondue, peas or beans.

Creamy fish dishes go with a piped border of duchesse potatoes and vegetables as for baked and poached fish.

Egg and Cheese dishes, Pâtés and terrines go with crisp bread or toast, green salad or tomato salad.

Meat and Poultry dishes go with all the hot vegetable dishes in this book, or served cold they go with all the salads. Green salad is particularly acceptable with roast beef and steaks.

Sweets are delicious with a sweet white Bordeaux or Burgundy. For a really expensive dessert wine, do not serve meringue or anything too sweet. A good fruit tart, fresh fruit, a soufflé omelette or Christmas pudding would off-set the wine better.

Temperature and Service. In general, red wines are served at room temperature, white wines slightly chilled. Most red wines improve by having the cork pulled an hour or two before service.

I once took on a student nurse to help in the restaurant. She was no good. She automatically shook the bottles before she poured out drinks. *Don't* shake up the wine!

If you aspire to being a wine drinker, go to a good merchant and buy a book on wines.

Beer and Stout are for informal meals. You could say that stout is for beef, steaks and stews; beer with pork, bacon and fowl; but it is very much to one's own taste.

INDEX